MW00571246

Mark Beckner, Dylan Jones
Upgrading and Migrating to BizTalk Server 20̲̲

Mark Beckner, Dylan Jones

Upgrading and Migrating to BizTalk Server 2016

——

DE
G
PRESS

ISBN 978-1-5015-1507-1
e-ISBN (PDF) 978-1-5015-0608-6
e-ISBN (EPUB) 978-1-5015-0601-7

Library of Congress Cataloging-in-Publication Data
A CIP catalog record for this book has been applied for at the Library of Congress.

Bibliographic information published by the Deutsche Nationalbibliothek
The Deutsche Nationalbibliothek lists this publication in the Deutsche Nationalbibliografie;
detailed bibliographic data are available on the Internet at http://dnb.dnb.de.

© 2017 Walter de Gruyter Inc., Boston/Berlin
Printing and binding: CPI book GmbH, Leck
♾ Printed on acid-free paper
Printed in Germany

www.degruyter.com

Acknowledgements

Thank you to my editor, Jeff Pepper, who has made it possible to publish on a variety of topics over a long period of time across several publishers.

Introduction

I was in the San Jose airport several days ago, and a fellow passenger on my flight noticed the backpack I was carrying. On it was the BizTalk 2010 logo – I've carried the backpack for seven years. He asked if I worked with BizTalk, and mentioned that he had heard of the product. The rest of the conversation was about other technologies; the only other mention of BizTalk was that he understood it to be an extremely complex server platform.

Several things stood out to me about this conversation.

First, I've traveled extensively over my career of 17-plus years, and this was the first time anyone ever asked me about BizTalk as a platform. BizTalk has always had a limited audience. There have been rumors since its inception that it was being discontinued. However, there are organizations that have implemented it and now depend on it. These organizations would be very hard pressed to find another platform that provides similar functionality. Very few organizations move away from BizTalk. Generally, once the platform is adopted, it stays.

Second, of those people who have heard of BizTalk, few have actually developed on it. It is a special skill set that can work with the product. Being able to work within an organization and know a platform that can be used to easily integrate internal systems or interact with external entities is a rare ability, and one that will allow you to work in a variety of capacities and with many systems and platforms. BizTalk and integration are both very valuable skills. Being able to converse across platforms and discuss how data can be shared continues to be very important.

BizTalk is a niche product, but its place in the Microsoft offerings has been rock solid. It is a platform that has lasted for 17 years, and will likely be around for many more. Knowing the full product is important, as each organization uses different components of it. Understanding the business rules engine, business activity monitoring, the use and configuration of the various adapters, and the EDI engine is important as a BizTalk developer.

I am certain that BizTalk won't generate another conversation for me in an airport in a very long time. But I am certain that there are organizations that need skilled people right now to help them with their BizTalk implementations. I know that many of these organizations need to upgrade to the latest version of BizTalk, and that many need to reexamine their solutions and update their code base. The topics in this book should provide approaches that will simplify these activities and help ensure the final result will last for years to come.

About the Author

Mark Beckner is a technical consultant specializing in business development and enterprise application integration. He runs Inotek Consulting Group, which delivers innovative solutions to large corporations and small businesses. His projects have included engagements with numerous clients throughout the U.S.

He has previously authored *Using Scribe Insight*, *BizTalk 2013 EDI for Health Care*, *BizTalk 2013 Recipes*, and *Microsoft Dynamics CRM API Development*, and has spoken at a number of venues. In addition to BizTalk, he works with Dyanmics 365, .NET, and an extensive list of platforms and technologies. Beckner, his wife, Sara, and his boys, Ciro and Iyer, live on a farm in western Colorado. His website is http://www.inotekgroup.com and he can be contacted directly at mbeckner@inotekgroup.com.

Contents

Chapter 1
Preparing for Your Upgrade

Every BizTalk migration and upgrade is different. This chapter outlines the key considerations that need to be taken into account when planning your migration, and includes details about performing the installation and configuration. You may have a solution that can be migrated virtually "as-is," or you may have something that will require some recoding and recompiling in order to get it to deploy properly. In either case, you will have an opportunity to examine your solution(s) in detail and make improvements before pushing into a brand-new BizTalk 2016 environment.

Upgrading to the new version of any enterprise application, such as BizTalk, is an opportunity not only to look at specifics of doing an in-place migration, but also looking at how to improve your solutions.

Migration Considerations

There is no way to know in advance exactly what will be required for any migration to BizTalk 2016 from an older version of BizTalk Server. Some solutions are very simple; some are very complex. Some will need to be recompiled with code updates, while others may be able to be migrated using the same compile code you already have. You will want to take all of the following into consideration as you plan your upgrade.

1. You must set up a brand-new BizTalk 2016 environment – new server(s), new database(s). There are no "in place" migrations of BizTalk. An overview of installing and configuring BizTalk 2016 is given later in this chapter.

2. In parallel with the first step, make sure you have the right licensing in place. We'll look at Standard Edition vs. Enterprise Edition licensing later in this chapter, in the section on licensing. This will also give an overview of the different server architectures that can be put into place using these different licenses.

3. It is possible that you can migrate your solution exactly as-is, without recompiling any DLLs. This is true even when migrating from BizTalk 2006. The compiled .NET code, in some cases, will work without any modification. We'll look at this in detail in Chapter 2. Your deployment may be as simple

DOI 10.1515/9781501506086-001

as exporting an MSI or a binding file, and deploying your .NET assemblies to the Global Assembly Cache (GAC).

In some cases, especially with a simple BizTalk solution, you can migrate compiled code to Biz-Talk 2016 exactly as-is without making any modifications. However, in most cases, you will need to make minor changes to maps, orchestrations, etc. and recompile these in Visual Studio 2015.

---

4. You'll want to decide how you move objects between environments. You can export an MSI and the associated Binding files, but these won't always be the best method to migrate. You may need to deploy some of your objects manually, while others use the imports of the exported MSIs. In cases where you are using Batching and complex party setups in an EDI solution, you may have to manually modify the binding files before importing. There are several scenarios outlined in Chapter 7 for how to deploy using different models.
5. You will want to take some time to consider if there are ways to improve your solution(s) prior to migrating. If, for example, you must recompile your code, you may want to take the opportunity to restructure your Visual Studio solution(s) and project(s). Often, developers will place all the code files for a Biz-Talk solution into a single project, making it very difficult to make changes or do deployments postproduction.

    Take a look at Figure 1.1 as an example of a single project with many maps. To make an update to a single map, you must recompile the entire project and deploy a large DLL. In a production setting, this would require impacting multiple running processes, and would be very cumbersome and stressful to work with. If your code is not split out into small, componentized structures (like those shown in the good example in Figure 1.2), then you should definitely spend some time rethinking this structure before deploying into a fresh new BizTalk 2016 environment. We'll cover this topic in more detail in Chapter 3.

Figure 1.1: A single monolithic project with many maps – an example of what NOT to do

Figure 1.2: Break your projects into small componentized units, rather than a monolithic structure

6. Look at simplifying your maps. Complex maps are very common in BizTalk, and first time BizTalk developers will often create exceptionally intricate maps that are extremely difficult to modify, test, and maintain. Using XSLT, C#, and other external technologies to the BizTalk UI Mapper is not only good practice, it can substantially reduce the amount of time to develop your maps. As you can see in Figure 1.3, using traditional functoids can create a very complex mapping environment. Additionally, there are a number of mapping scenarios that simply cannot be solved through using the standard functoids.

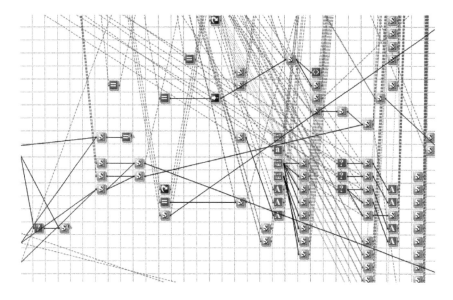

Figure 1.3: Using standard functoids can cause unreadable and unsupportable maps

You will want to make sure that you can develop in XSLT, which will ensure that you can solve every mapping scenario and also keep your maps easy to read and update (see Figure 1.4). More information on mapping can be found in the mapping discussions in Chapter 3, and the .NET and SQL utilization discussions in Chapter 4.

Your migration is the best time to examine how you can simplify your existing maps, and how you can create a new paradigm for future mapping work that you may do. You must learn to incorporate XSLT into your mapping options.

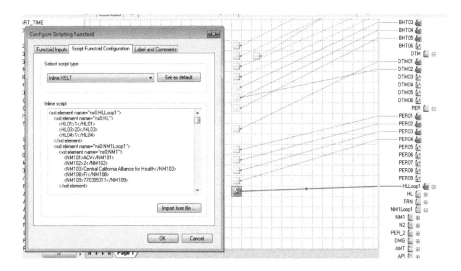

Figure 1.4: Incorporating XSLT can greatly simply your mapping environment

7. Try to eliminate complex orchestrations and delivery patterns. In many cases, what might have been developed 10 years ago on BizTalk 2006 may work more or less "as is" when upgrading to BizTalk 2016, but the architecture is grossly outdated. There are patterns available that can take what required multiple maps and orchestrations the first time around and replace it with only a very finite number of well-constructed and simple-to-build BizTalk components.

   If you open your Visual Studio solution and are unable to immediately piece together how components interact, or you look at your BizTalk Admin console and don't fully understand how things have been deployed and how your integrations are working, then you must take the time to piece all of it together. You should take advantage of that work and use that time to come up with a simpler model for your upgraded environment. Chapter 3 has more information about simplifying orchestrations.

8. You will need to plan appropriately for resourcing and costs associated with your migration. In some cases, you'll be able to do this with a minimum of effort – but in most cases, you will need to set aside a substantial amount of time to work through this and complete it with success. Chapter 6 will give more detail about how to approach resourcing around your migration.

Take the time to do a proper assessment of the time it will take to do your BizTalk migration. There may be more (or less!) to it than you think. In a matter of a few hours, a BizTalk expert should be able to come up with a fairly accurate estimate of time and costs.

---

9. Look at what options may be available in utilizing Azure. Many corporations are looking at ways to push things to the cloud. BizTalk was the original platform that Azure was born from, and there is a lot of talk about BizTalk in the cloud. Understand what is available, and how the various models might make sense for you. Chapter 5 outlines options and considerations around BizTalk and Azure.

While there are a number of other things that may come to mind as you plan your migration, these are the most critical considerations. Given everything you must consider, the first step is to have a BizTalk 2016 environment where you can experiment with your current codebase and see how various aspects of it will migrate. Therefore, the very first thing you will want to do is get your new BizTalk 2016 environment up and running.

BizTalk 2016 Licensing and Installation

You must install BizTalk in a new environment. There is no option for an "in place" migration, as there is for many other platforms. You must stand BizTalk 2016 up in a new environment and move all your code to that new environment. Therefore, the most logical first step in preparing for your migration is getting a new server infrastructure set up, configured, and installed. BizTalk consists of two primary components – the application server, which is where BizTalk and any related code components are installed (such as DLLs, WCF services, etc.), and the SQL Server database server, where all the BizTalk databases are created.

Very little has changed with the installation of BizTalk Server 2016 from previous editions. We'll walk through a basic installation and configuration in a moment, but before you do an installation, take some time to think about the options available to you. It may be time to give your solution a boost in performance and availability, or, conversely, it may be time to scale back the resources you've dedicated to it in the past.

The cost of BizTalk licenses has changed with BizTalk 2016, and is based on a per-core model. Figure 1.5 shows the current pricing as the time of this writing. You can find out more at https://www.microsoft.com/en-us/cloud-platform/biztalk-pricing.

BizTalk pricing

Edition	Primary usage scenario	Estimated price (USD)*
Enterprise	For customers with enterprise-level requirements for high volume, reliability, and availability	$10,835 per core license
Standard	For organizations with moderate volume and deployment scale requirements	$2,485 per core license
Branch	Specialty version of BizTalk Server designed for hub and spoke deployment scenarios, including RFID	$620 per core license
Developer	For MSDN subscription holders looking to test and develop on the platform (Not licensed for production use)	N/A

*Estimated reseller pricing under the Microsoft Volume Licensing Open NL program is provided for demonstrative purposes only. Actual pricing may vary based on reseller and/or geographical location.

Figure 1.5: A screenshot of the current Microsoft BizTalk license pricing

The Simple Standard Edition Solution

Standard Edition is a cheap-license and an easy-deployment model. For small-scale integrations that do not require real-time or highly available implementations, the Standard Edition can be a cost-effective way to get BizTalk into your environment. When migrating, you may find that the original license you purchased was an Enterprise Edition license, but you never really used the benefits of this license. For example, many organizations will have a single BizTalk application server with the Enterprise Edition installed on it. The core reason to have the Enterprise Edition is to scale out your architecture and have multiple BizTalk Group boxes sharing load.

If you have only a single server, or a dual server (BizTalk and SQL) architecture, you likely only need BizTalk Standard Edition. You may have to reorganize your BizTalk applications so that you have only five, but this is a small effort, and using Standard over Enterprise can lead to sizable cost savings.

There are two models that you can have with BizTalk Standard Edition. The first, shown in Figure 1.6, is a single box with both BizTalk and SQL installed on it. This architecture is recommended only in a development or test scenario. In this scenario, you usually have Visual Studio as well as other development tools in place. Only in cases where your company is very small and you have limited funds or hardware availability should this model be used in a production setting.

BizTalk App and
SQL DB Server

Figure 1.6: Single Server Standard Edition used in a development setting

A production environment with BizTalk Standard Edition should be based on the second model, shown in Figure 1.7. In this model, the BizTalk application server is separated from the SQL database server. This ensures that the load on the CPU is balanced more effectively, and allows you to license and structure the RAM and CPUs on both boxes appropriately. For example, many BizTalk implementations use far more system resources on the SQL box than they do on the BizTalk box. Therefore, you may be able to create a solution where you have a BizTalk Server with two CPUs (and therefore are paying only for that cost) and a SQL Server with four CPUs (and are paying that for the SQL licenses). There is a lot of flexibility in how you configure your boxes and what type of licensing is proper for you.

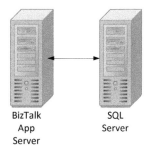

Figure 1.7: Dual Server Standard Edition

The Standard Edition is often overlooked when organizations look to purchase BizTalk. Generally, this is because of the idea that it will handle only "five applications." An application in BizTalk is not the same as a separate unit of work, and does not mean that you will be limited to only five solutions – really, it is more like a file directory and an organizational tool than anything else. Figure 1.8 shows where these applications are located. You can deploy anything you want within a single application, even integrations that have nothing in common.

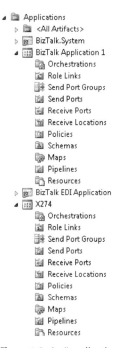

Figure 1.8: An "application" in BizTalk is just an organizational tool

Prior to migrating your older BizTalk solution – which may be on the Enterprise Edition – take time to look at Standard and see if you can fit your solution into this cheaper pricing model.

The Simple Multi-Server Enterprise Edition Solution

The Enterprise Edition allows for multiple BizTalk boxes to be added to a BizTalk Group. A group is one or more servers that share load across each-other – similar to a SQL cluster. If you have two servers in a group, the second one will process data when the first one is consumed. There is no exact science to when one Biz-Talk box within the group will take over from the other, but the basic concept is that if one server is under load, the second server will pick up newly inbound processes. And – if one of the servers in the group fails, there is no impact to your running processes, as the other server will continue to process. Figure 1.9 shows a simple multi-server environment where two BizTalk servers are part of a single Group and share a single SQL Server database.

A new server can be added to a BizTalk Group at any time. This means that if you have low load the first year, and your requirements change in the second year, you can add the second server to the group at that time.

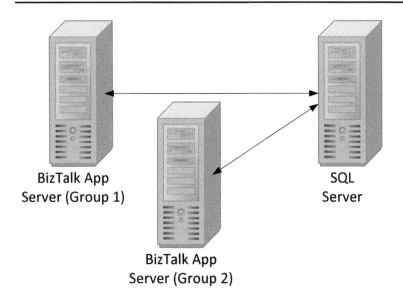

BizTalk App
Server (Group 1)

SQL
Server

BizTalk App
Server (Group 2)

Figure 1.9: Basic Multi-Server Enterprise Edition

The Highly Available Enterprise Edition Solution with SQL Clustering

The simple BizTalk multi-server environment shown above in Figure 1.9 is an extremely common production solution, and is often thought of as being highly available. This is not accurate. It is only highly available in the sense that if one of the BizTalk Servers goes down, the other one will continue to run. However, the database is still a single point of failure. So, it is only halfway to the "highly available" target. To get true failover availability, clustering SQL Server is a requirement. This model is shown in Figure 1.10.

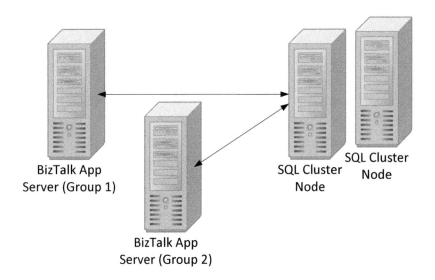

Figure 1.10: Multi-Server Enterprise Edition in Clustered SQL Environment – High Availability

Notes on Web Services

One other item to take into consideration is external facing apps that may be part of your BizTalk solution, but are built on different technologies. The best example of this is the use of web services. BizTalk orchestrations can be published as web services, which will create proxy web service files in the local BizTalk Server's Internet Information Server (IIS). In a highly available BizTalk environment, shown above in Figure 1.11, the IIS portion of the solution is highly available only if there is some sort of web load balancer sitting in front of the two BizTalk boxes brokering requests. Each box has its own IP and name, so each would have its own web URL for external apps to call. If you have no load balancing, then applications would have to reference either the first box or the second box directly, as shown in Figure 1.11.

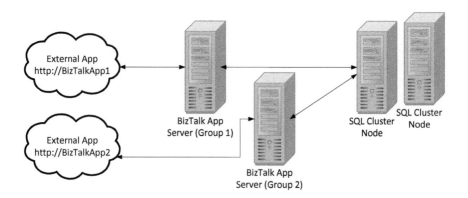

Figure 1.11: Non-Highly Available Web Architecture – Single Point of Failure at IIS Level

For this web portion of the solution to be highly available, a load balancer or similar would be required. This load balancer would translate a single URL request and rotate it to each of the servers on the backend, something like the architecture shown in Figure 1.12. The external apps hit a single URL; that URL is then split to the individual backend BizTalk boxes through the load balancer's configuration. New BizTalk boxes added to the group can then share load in the future by simply adding them into the Web Balancer's list of boxes to send requests to.

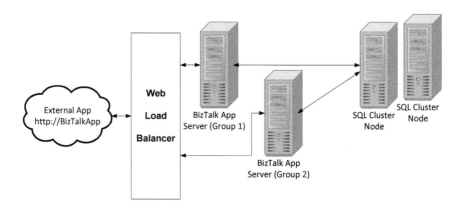

Figure 1.12: Highly Available Web Architecture – No Single Points of Failure

Exercise: BizTalk 2016 Installation and Configuration

This exercise will walk you through the basic installation and configuration for BizTalk Server 2016. There are several patterns available to you in an installation, the most common of which are the single-server install used in a development/testing environment and a multi-server install used in a production environment. Both are very similar in the steps taken during the install and configuration. The section that follows the walkthrough demonstrated below will note those things you must consider when deploying in a multi-server environment.

Installation

The installation of the BizTalk software is very easy and usually takes about 30 minutes to complete. Once you click on the Setup executable, you have several options – allowing the setup utility to automatically download and install the prerequisites is the ideal option. If for some reason, you have heavy security on your box, and Internet Explorer is set to not allow downloads, you will have to download these files on a separate computer that has access to the internet and then transfer them manually to the server where you are installing BizTalk. The installation of the prerequisite files is shown in Figure 1.13.

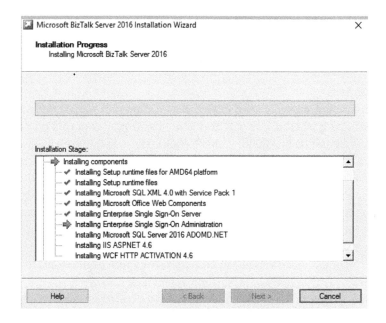

Figure 1.13: Installing the prerequisite components required by the BizTalk application

Once the required components have been installed, the installation wizard will move on to install the core BizTalk engine and files. There isn't much to do for the installation other than watch it progress. The real work comes in the configuration of BizTalk. When the installation is complete, the wizard will prompt you to start the configuration, as shown in Figure 1.14. If you miss this or want to do the configuration at a later time, you can access the BizTalk Server Configuration application via your Start menu.

Figure 1.14: Once the installation completes, you can start the configuration

Configuration Options

The initial configuration screen (shown in Figure 1.15) allows for several things. The first is determining whether you will be doing a basic or custom configuration. The basic configuration installs all of the BizTalk components, which is generally unnecessary for most organizations. For example, not every organization will use BAM or EDI or the BizTalk Rules Engine. The basic configuration should be used only for a development environment and only in a single-server setup (where the database and BizTalk application sit on the same server). The custom configuration is for multi-server setups (where you have a minimum of two servers, the database server and the BizTalk application server separated from one another) and for configurations where you need to have control over groups, users, and permissions (virtually every production deployment).

The next item to determine is the database server name where the BizTalk databases will be installed. BizTalk installs a number of databases, depending on which options in the configuration you select. In a production environment, you will want to have a dedicated BizTalk database server. In a development or test environment, you can share a database server that has other databases installed on it. Only one version of BizTalk can be installed on any single database instance; for example, you cannot use the same database instance for your BizTalk 2016 environment as you would for your BizTalk 2010 instance from which you may be upgrading.

The final item you will need to determine is the service account you will use. In a production environment, or any multi-server install, you will need to set up a number of Windows domain groups and users, one of which will be a BizTalk service account (usually called something like BTService). This is the account that all the services will run under (in Windows Services), and which will be used to log these services into the underlying databases. The full list of Windows users and groups that will need to be set up can be found in a number of places, including the following link.

https://msdn.microsoft.com/en-us/library/aa577661.aspx

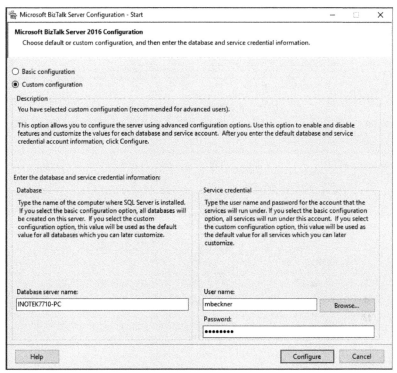

Figure 1.15: Initial configuration screen

Configuring Enterprise SSO

When accessing the numerous systems across a network that are common in an integration environment, there are many security credentials that most likely will be necessary. Even in a multi-server environment where BizTalk must access its own databases from multiple BizTalk Group servers, management of security is an issue. Enterprise Single Sign on (SSO) is BizTalk's tool for managing these credentials and security domains. In 99% of BizTalk configurations, configuring this is the only time you as an administrator or developer will ever see SSO. Enterprise SSO can be used to store and manage credentials that allow BizTalk to access systems across the network. However, a much easier and arguably just as secure method is to store these credentials in the BizTalk configuration file. Configuring SSO is shown in Figure 1.16.

A new server can be added to a BizTalk Group at any time. This means that if you have low load the first year, and your requirements change in the second year, you can add the second server to the group at that time.

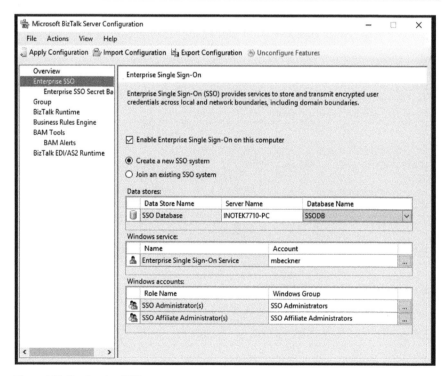

Figure 1.16: Configuring SSO

Configuring the BizTalk Group

When using the Enterprise Edition of BizTalk Server, you have the option to add one or more BizTalk application servers to the group. The first group server configured must use the "Create a new BizTalk Group" option, as shown in Figure 1.17. The second group server must run the BizTalk configuration tool separately and select the "Join an existing BizTalk Group" option.

When adding a second BizTalk server to an existing BizTalk group, you will need to run the BizTalk configuration tool from that second (or third, etc.) server. You will not need to configure anything except the group settings (where you will "Join" an existing group), as the rest of the environment has already been configured.

Note that with the Standard Edition, you will only be able to have a single BizTalk Group box in your environment – only Enterprise Edition allows for multiple servers within a group.

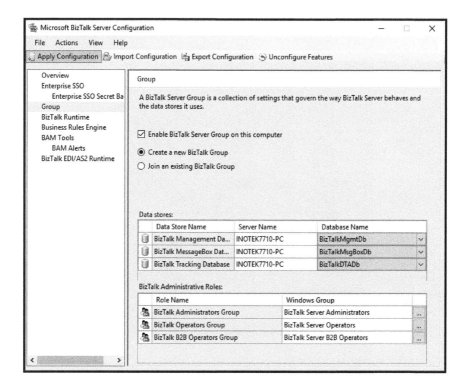

Figure 1.17: Configuring the BizTalk Group

Configuring the BizTalk Runtime

This portion of the configuration can be a little confusing, but it is basically set-ting up the host instance information that will be used to run the BizTalk adapt-ers, orchestrations, and any other component deployed within BizTalk. The most common configuration is shown in Figure 1.18. These settings can be altered once the configuration is complete by accessing the hosts and host instances within the BizTalk Administration tool. You may also create additional hosts that can be used to separate adapters, applications, etc.

In a highly available environment, there are some adapters that will instantiate on each BizTalk server if using the default BizTalk host. For example, if you are using the SQL adapter and have a receive port deployed using the default Host instance, it will trigger simultaneously on both servers, resulting in your solution executing twice. There are several solutions to this, the easi-est of which is to create a host application that runs on only one of the servers and tying this adapter to that host application.

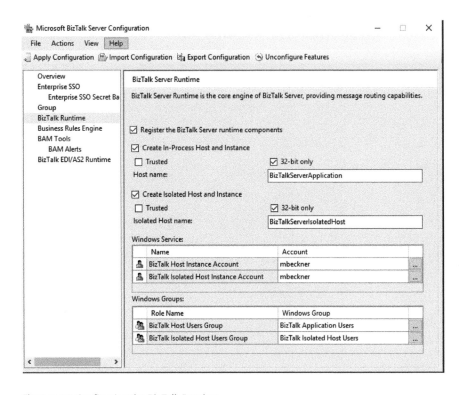

Figure 1.18: Configuring the BizTalk Runtime

Configuring the Business Rules Engine

One of my least favorite tools within BizTalk is the Business Rules Engine (BRE). The concept is great, but the implementation is poor, difficult to work with, and often results in very complex solutions that are difficult to maintain and extend. My experience has taught me that virtually any scenario where a configurable rule or property is required can most easily be done through a C# helper library or intelligent logic within the database tier. If you have a solution that uses the BRE and you are looking at migrating it to BizTalk 2016, you may want to migrate things exactly as they are, and therefore use the BRE. But, if you are considering new development or have the opportunity to rethink your architecture during your migration, eliminating the BRE would be my recommendation.

Creating your own approach to managing business rules is generally a better option than using the BizTalk Business Rules Engine. You can do some amazing work using database components that are easy to develop and can be maintained by far more developers than the BRE.

Configuring Business Activity Monitoring (BAM)

Another overly complex aspect to BizTalk that often leads to unintended and un-necessary complexity is BAM. Getting at metrics and analyzing your custom so-lutions can be done in so many ways that BAM is generally unnecessary. You can create your own logic to track where a process is and push it into more common reporting tools like SQL Server Reporting Services (SSRS) or existing reporting frameworks that your organization already has. I generally enable BAM only when working with EDI and AS2 solutions. There is some good reporting you can get out of the box for applications using these engines. But for solutions I build for clients, I always work to tie in reporting to something they are already familiar with and can easily configure and modify.

Architecting your integrations to tie in with existing reporting and analysis technologies that your organization already uses is your best option.

Configuring EDI and AS2

Many BizTalk environments have no use for the EDI engine. If you are using EDI within your environment, you'll need to enable the Runtime, as shown in Figure 1.19. AS2 is a rare need, but if you will be doing direct AS2 transactions with trad-ing partners, you will want to enable this piece of the solution. Some extended reporting is available if you have BAM installed (which requires SQL Server Analysis Services). If you want this, you'll select the third option shown in the figure.

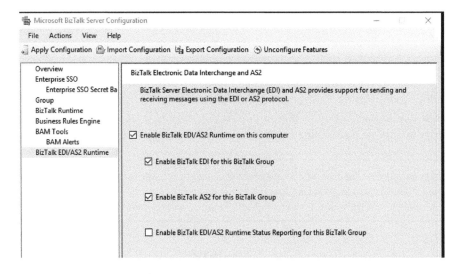

Figure 1.19: Configuring EDI and AS2

Notes on Configurations within a Multi-Server Environment

When installing BizTalk on multiple servers, several items differ from single-server configurations. The key differences are as follows:

1. You must use Windows domain groups and users (on a single-server instance you can use local Windows accounts). This has been covered in an earlier section within this chapter.

2. You will need to enable Microsoft Distributed Transaction Coordinator on all servers. MSDTC is used to ensure communications to and from the database to the BizTalk Group application servers can be completed or rolled back, depending on the interruptions in the network or other connectivity. To enable MSDTC, you must open Component Services and click on the Properties of DTC, as shown in Figure 1.20. Once the MSDTC property window has opened, you will need to set the properties as shown in Figure 1.21.

The MSDTC settings must be set identically on each of the boxes within the BizTalk environment. This includes the SQL database server(s) and the BizTalk Group server(s).

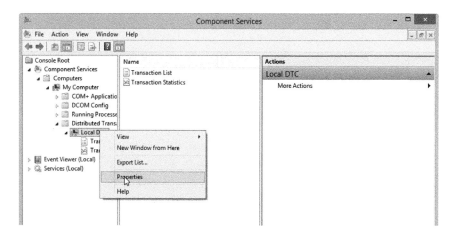

Figure 1.20: Accessing MSDTC

Tracing	Logging	Security

Security Settings

☑ Network DTC Access

Client and Administration

☑ Allow Remote Clients   ☑ Allow Remote Administration

Transaction Manager Communication

☑ Allow Inbound   ☑ Allow Outbound

○ Mutual Authentication Required

○ Incoming Caller Authentication Required

⦿ No Authentication Required

☑ Enable XA Transactions   ☑ Enable SNA LU 6.2 Transactions

DTC Logon Account

Account: NT AUTHORITY\NetworkService   [Browse...]

Password:

Confirm password:

Learn more about setting these properties.

[OK] [Cancel] [Apply]

Figure 1.21: Configuring EDI and AS2

Notes on SQL Server Maintenance

SQL Server maintenance is often an afterthought in a BizTalk deployment. Make sure you are conscious of it, and are treating it as any other SQL database on your network. Truncating tables and log files, monitoring disk usage and overall health – anything you do for other databases needs to be done for the BizTalk databases. There is nothing special about these databases, and in many cases they can be left untouched for years without impact. However, there are several things to be aware of and to address, as shown in the following list.

You should have SQL database administrators assigned to your BizTalk installation so that they are familiar with it from the start. Many database administrators will ignore BizTalk SQL databases, because they are unfamiliar with BizTalk. The general rule of thumb is to maintain and monitor your BizTalk databases just as you would any other SQL Server environment within your network.

---

1. Some applications, such as large-scale EDI implementations, will use a tremendous amount of disk space. The actual amount will vary based on tracking settings enabled on application, ports, orchestrations, etc. and the type of server architecture you have (multi-server environments will have different tracking and database usage than single servers). Make sure you are monitoring for database and log file growth, and that you have some plan for truncating data and log files when they get very large.
2. There are several SQL jobs that should be enabled. These are installed by default with BizTalk, but are not enabled. You'll want to turn all the BizTalk jobs on. If you experience any performance issues, you can turn these off – they are not mission critical, and can be left off for long periods of time. They handle database cleanup, especially the elimination of unneeded messages from the MessageBox database. Figure 1.22 shows the BizTalk jobs interspersed with other jobs unrelated to BizTalk. Your environment will vary, but you can easily pick out the BizTalk-specific jobs. Make sure and monitor the history of these for any exceptions that may be thrown.

Figure 1.22: BizTalk SQL Jobs should be enabled and monitored

Summary

You should at this point have a firm idea of what you want to accomplish in your migration. You will be installing and configuring BizTalk in a new server environment, and must decide if you want a simple architecture or one that is highly available. When you move your solution, you'll have to decide if you want to keep it exactly as it has been programmed to date or if you'll be re-architecting it to better use available technology and better align with your business. There are many things to consider and experimenting with the code in a BizTalk 2016 environment will be your best litmus test for how much work will be required in your migration. In Chapter 2, we will begin looking at this process of experimentation.

Chapter 2
Migrating Your Solution

In Chapter 1, you looked through all the considerations that need to be taken into account before upgrading your solutions to BizTalk 2016. You also worked through the installation and configuration of a new BizTalk 2016 server environment. With the 2016 environment set up, and those considerations taken into account, you are now ready to work through a deployment of your solutions. This chapter will walk you through various deployment techniques that you can use to deploy your code.

Working through a deployment of your code as an early step in your migration is good practice. It will allow you to get something in place to begin unit testing your components and seeing which of these components may need code updates. As noted in the first chapter, you may find that your solution will migrate exactly as-is, without making any modifications.

Jumping right into deploying your code in a BizTalk 2016 environment is the quickest way to understanding how much recoding may be necessary with your maps, orchestrations, and other components.

Planning Your Deployment

In order to most easily deploy, you need to determine the smallest unit of your solution that will be able to stand alone in the new environment. For example, let's say that your old BizTalk 2010 environment consists of two integrations; the first is an orchestration exposed as a SOAP web service, while the second is an EDI solution that receives an EDI document from an FTP site, maps the file to an XML doc, and pushes that XML doc to a database using a stored procedure. These are very different solutions, and can be deployed separate from one another. The first could be deployed and set up to be fully functional on the new 2016 server, while the second could remain running on the old 2010 server. They are not interdependent, and therefore should be migrated separately.

The deployment options for both scenarios and virtually any other BizTalk solution are as follows:
1. You can do a manual deployment of ports, parties, compiled .NET assemblies, and other components.

DOI 10.1515/9781501506086-002

2. You can export your MSI and binding files and import these into the new 2016 environment, letting these imports set up the ports, orchestrations, and configurations, while you manually deploy the .NET assemblies to the Global Assembly Cache (GAC).

3. You can deploy any non-BizTalk components, such as web service proxy services within IIS, referenced BizTalk assemblies, etc. manually.

For BizTalk 2006, 2006 R2, 2010, and 2013, you will have very similar issues to work through in your upgrade regardless of the version you are migrating from. BizTalk 2004 most likely need to be rewritten from scratch, as it is unlikely that your assemblies and applications will have any component that can be deployed "as-is." BizTalk 2000 and 2002 are ancient technology, and your solutions must be rewritten completely – you are not looking at a migration, but rather a full rewrite.

You will most likely need to do a combination of all three of these options, depending on the complexity of your solutions. Some solutions you may want to migrate entirely by hand because of their architectural simplicity. Others, such as those that use EDI batching orchestrations and large numbers of BizTalk Parties, will require manual intervention at the batch level and the importing of bindings to create the various party settings.

We'll now look at these various deployment methods in more detail. In each of these models, any deployment of .NET assemblies (DLLs) should be first done with the already compiled code you have deployed in your old BizTalk environment. Trying the deployment with these pre-compiled DLLs will give you a baseline for understanding what will need to be done for your final migration.

Start your migration with pre-compiled DLLs. Wait to recompile your .NET code (which includes all of the BizTalk project code as well as helper class libraries) in a newer version of Visual Studio until you see what upgrades without being touched.

Manual Deployments

When you have a live production environment, and you need to roll out a map update or some other code fix in a .NET assembly, the easiest and least risky approach is a manual deployment. You need to know how to do this for your migration as well, as no matter what level of MSI automation you may have, there will still be times that you'll want to register things separately in the GAC.

All BizTalk artifacts within a Visual Studio solution compile into a .NET assembly. Physical copies of these assemblies are required for a manual deployment. If you do not have a physical copy of the file, you can either recompile these in either the original version of Visual Studio that was compatible with the version of BizTalk you are migrating from, or within Visual Studio 2015 for BizTalk 2016. You can also try and copy them out of the GAC. You should be able to navigate to them via some path (depending on your operating system) similar to C:\Windows\Microsoft.NET\assembly\GAC_32. You can view items in the assembly at C:\Windows\assembly, but you generally cannot copy directly out of this directory.

Taking the example of the orchestration exposed as a web service mentioned earlier, there are several steps to a manual deployment. In this case, you have one assembly (.NET DLL) that contains the BizTalk orchestrations, schemas, and/or maps, one referenced "Helper" assembly that is referred to from within the orchestration, and one web service proxy that must be deployed and configured within IIS. The following steps outline what is needed for the manual deployment of this example.

1. First, create an Application in BizTalk where you will deploy the components. Note that you do NOT need a special application for this. You can create one, or you can use an existing one (such as the default "BizTalk Application 1" available when you first open the Administration Console). For now, you can name this application the same as what you have in your old BizTalk environment.

2. Next, right-click this application and select Add and then BizTalk Assemblies, as shown in Figure 2.1. This will allow you to select one or more assemblies to deploy within this application.

   A good rule to follow here is to click the "Overwrite All" checkbox. This applies to every assembly and ensures that whatever you are deploying overwrites any previous deployment of the same assembly. Then, click on each individual assembly you are deploying in the list and click on the first and third checkboxes (see Figure 2.2). This will force a deployment not only to the BizTalk databases but also to the GAC. All assemblies must reside in the GAC, and this is a simple way to guarantee that they are there. Any referenced .NET assemblies (such as the "Helper" assembly used in this example) should be included in this deployment. This process will register them in the GAC, and ensure that they can be referenced by the orchestration when they run.

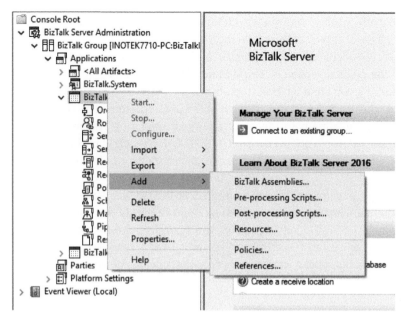

Figure 2.1: Manually deploying assemblies from the BizTalk Administration Console

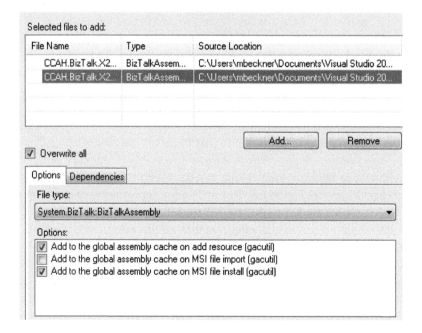

Figure 2.2: Setting the appropriate options on each of the assemblies being added

3. With the assemblies deployed to BizTalk, you now can create the ports. In the case of the orchestration deployed as a web service, you will have a two-way receive port. Setting this up manually is just a matter of transferring the port configurations in your current production BizTalk environment to your new BizTalk 2016 environment.

    Copying and pasting each individual setting (as shown in Figure 2.3) is a quick-and-dirty way to get these ports set properly. On the left side of the image is a remote desktop instance where the old version of BizTalk is pulled up. On the right side, the new BizTalk 2016 Administration Console is open – values are copied from the left and pasted in the right.

    While this approach is fine for a handful of ports, you can see how it would not be sustainable for large solutions. This is where the importing of bindings, outlined later in this chapter, will become vital to your upgrade.

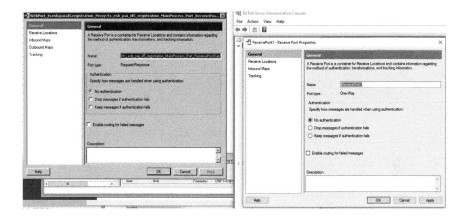

Figure 2.3: Copying current settings from Production (on the left) to the new BizTalk 2016 server (on the right)

4. Next, you will need to update the BizTalk configuration file with any custom configurable keys that may have been added. This file is named BTSNTSvc.exe.config, and is found in the root BizTalk installation folder in Windows Explorer. In this scenario, the Helper assembly calls a SQL database, and this database connection string is pulled from the configuration file. An example of the configuration file with the configurable <appSettings> node is shown in Figure 2.4.

Some BizTalk solutions will use the SSO tools to store configurable data. You can continue to use this model, or you can migrate your configurable fields to the BizTalk configuration file for simplicity. You will have to manually migrate these settings from your old SSO database to your new one – most likely by using the SSO Application Configuration tool in 2016.

Figure 2.4: Remember to copy any <appSettings> in the BizTalk configuration file

Remember that when you make modifications to the BizTalk configuration file, you will need to restart the BizTalk host instance. This can be done via the BizTalk Administration Console under the Platform Settings/Host Instances folder.

5. You can now deploy the proxy web service code to IIS. The code folder can be copied from your existing web directory (most likely under C:\inetpub\wwwroot) to your new BizTalk 2016 server. Once the folder is copied and pasted, open IIS and make sure you have an Application Pool created that will run under the correct .NET framework. In this case, the original web services were SOAP based, and they ran under .NET 2.0. You can continue to run them under .NET 2.0 in the new environment to ensure compatibility. At some point, you may want to publish this orchestration as a WCF service to modernize it, but at this stage in your manual migration, you don't need to introduce new pieces of functionality outside of BizTalk when you are just working to see if your core BizTalk artifacts will work without modification.

In addition to the Application Pool, you will also need to right-click your folder and select "Convert to Application." This will allow you to set the App Pool this proxy web service will run under and the permissions it will use when called. An example of this configuration is shown in Figure 2.5.

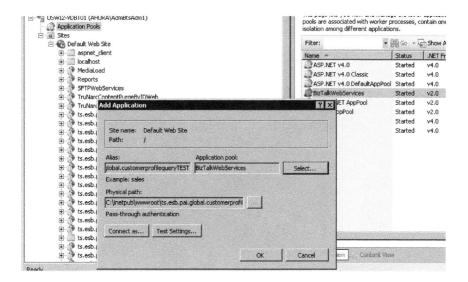

Figure 2.5: Settings in IIS for the SOAP Web Service

MSI Deployments

The previous section on manual deployments gives you full control over exactly what is happening with your deployment, but it isn't realistic for large-scale solutions with many BizTalk artifacts. To deal with larger implementations, you will want to use MSI files. You can export an MSI for your current environment and import it into your new environment. The MSI can contain one or more applications, and each application can contain all the BizTalk artifacts. This can save substantial time and ease your migration when compared with migrating one artifact at a time manually as described in the previous section.

You do not need to run the MSI on BizTalk; you only need to import it. Many people think that the BizTalk MSI is like other installer MSI packages. In this case, it should only be used to import into BizTalk, and not double-clicked and run like an executable.

Exporting the MSI

To begin with, you will need to export your MSI from your existing old BizTalk Server. This exported file, once created, will be imported into your new BizTalk 2016 environment. You can do this by right-clicking the BizTalk application you want to migrate within the BizTalk Administration Console and selecting Export and MSI file, as shown in Figure 2.6. While you can export an MSI for more than a single application, it makes it much easier to troubleshoot and pinpoint issues when you do it application by application.

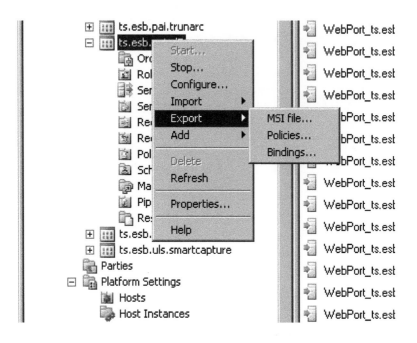

Figure 2.6: Exporting an MSI file from the BizTalk Admin Console

The MSI file export option will open a dialogue box that is the beginning of several pages of options within the MSI export wizard. On the Select Resources page, you will want to make sure you are selecting all the assemblies, as shown in Figure 2.7. As this image shows, both the referenced .NET helper assemblies (which do not contain BizTalk artifacts, but are referenced by those artifacts) and the core BizTalk assemblies that contain the schemas, pipelines, maps, and orchestrations. You will also want to select the Global Party Bindings (shown in Figure 2.8) if you are using EDI or BizTalk parties in any capacity.

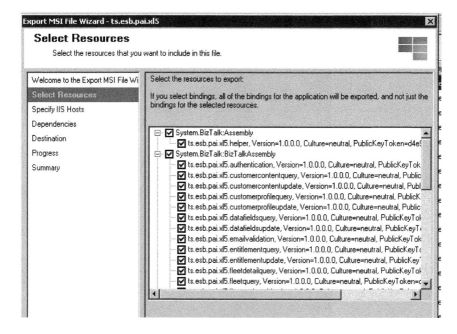

Figure 2.7: Selecting the .NET assemblies

You will still want to import your bindings file separately after you have imported the MSI. See the section later in this chapter on binding files.

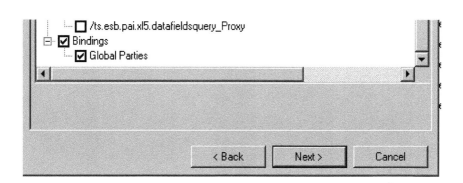

Figure 2.8: Selecting the bindings

You will NOT want to import any of the Web Resources. You'll want to deploy these manually – by copying your web directories from your old server and pasting and configuring them in IIS on your new server. Look at Step 5 in the manual deployment earlier in this chapter. Importing these automatically via the MSI can be a challenge, and can be very time consuming to get the configurations right, whereas copying and pasting is quick and ensures that you are setting the right permissions in the new environment. Figure 2.9 is a reminder to not include these in your MSI export.

Make sure you do not include web resources in your MSI export. You should handle this migration manually by copying and pasting the web proxy folders from your old server to your new server and using IIS to configure permissions and access.

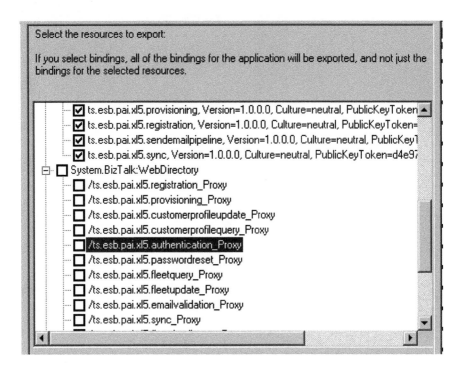

Figure 2.9: Do not include the Web Directory proxy files

The next screen in the wizard – titled Specify IIS Hosts – should have no information in it, as you are not exporting your web directories in the MSI. While you can certainly try to get these to import, if you have anything other than an empty screen showing (like Figure 2.10), then you'll have quite a bit of additional work to get them to import properly in your new environment.

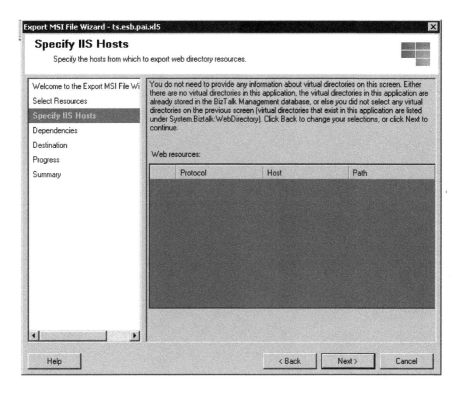

Figure 2.10: It is best to manually deploy web components and NOT include them in the MSI export

The Dependencies screen comes up next, giving a summary of what other applications are referenced by your application. Anything referenced here must already be on your target BizTalk environment before you'll be able to import this MSI. In the case of the application shown in Figure 2.11, the only application referenced is System.BizTalk, which is the root BizTalk engine. In this case, because System.BizTalk already exists in the target environment, your application can be imported. If it were referencing another application not already in the target environment, you would need to migrate the root application first.

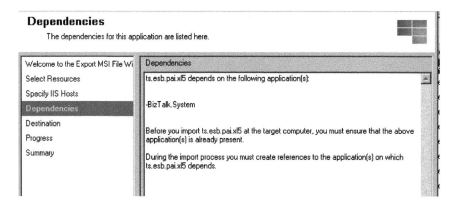

Figure 2.11: Showing what other applications are referenced by your application

You can see what applications are referenced by right-clicking your application in the BizTalk Admin Console and clicking Properties. There is a References tab that shows referenced applications, as shown in Figure 2.12.

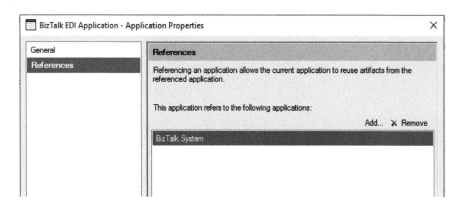

Figure 2.12: Refer to the References tab for required applications

Back in the export wizard, the final configurable step of the MSI export is defining the application name and determining where the output MSI will go. You will want to create an application in the BizTalk 2016 environment with a name that matches what you type in here (see the "Destination application name" property in Figure 2.13). After you have this set, and the path for the exported MSI file defined, you can click through the rest of the wizard to create the MSI file.

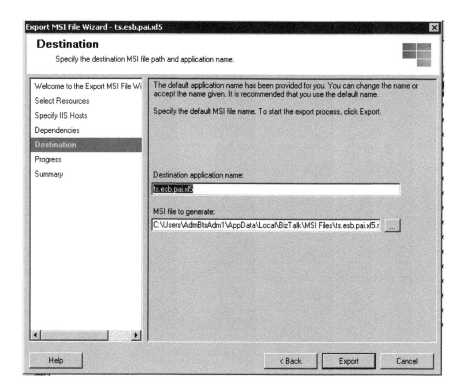

Figure 2.13: Setting the application name and exported file location

When the MSI file is completely exported, you'll next need to export the binding file. This can be done by right-clicking the application in the BizTalk Admin Console and selecting Export and Bindings. The dialogue box shown in Figure 2.14 will appear. Your bindings represent all the port configurations related to this application. If, for example, you have a send port writing to a location on your C: drive, then this C: drive location will be output into the binding file.

Additionally, the bindings allow you to export the Global Party information, which includes all the party configurations you might have. In EDI-centric solutions, this is the core of your solution. Know that everything except the batching information is included in the bindings. The batches, if you have them configured, need to be manually validated and started in your new environment.

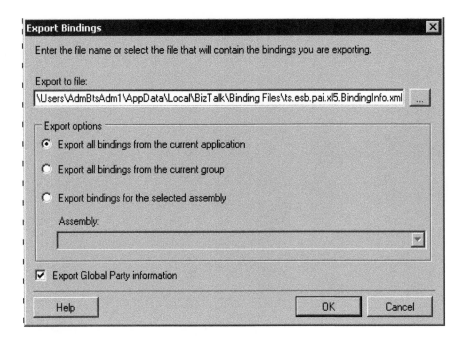

Figure 2.14: Exporting the bindings for your application

Importing the MSI

Take the MSI and the binding files you have exported, and copy them to the new BizTalk 2016 server. You will also need to copy the compiled assemblies used in the application, as these will need to be deployed to the GAC on the 2016 server. See Step 2 in the Manual Deployment section earlier in this chapter for information on how these will be imported. You will want to do this adding of the assemblies to the GAC after the import of the MSI and binding files has completed.

If you cannot find the original DLLs that you have deployed, and you can't copy them out of the GAC as described earlier in this chapter, you have two choices. The first is to compile them in the original version of Visual Studio that you used for the old version of BizTalk you are exporting from. If you find that there are many errors when you try to build your solution, skip the troubleshooting and recompile them in a newer version of Visual Studio, supported by BizTalk 2016 (like VS 2015).

In the BizTalk 2016 Admin Console, right-click the application that you will be importing your MSI into. If you need to create a new one, do so now. On the right-click context menu, select Import and MSI. This will open an import wizard, the first page of which is shown in Figure 2.15. On this screen, you will want to browse to the MSI file that you just exported from your older version of BizTalk.

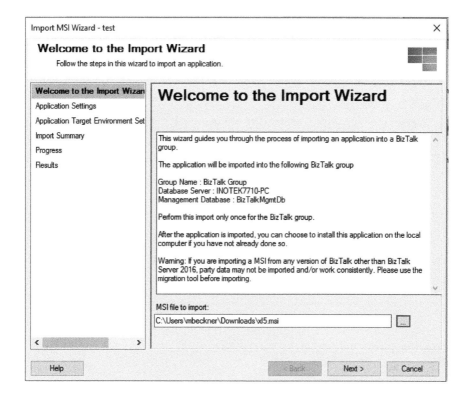

Figure 2.15: Starting the import wizard

On the second screen of the import wizard, which is the Application Settings page (see Figure 2.16), you determine what applications will be referenced (you should be able to use the defaults, although if you have an application being referenced not in 2016, you won't be able to import your MSI). You also determine if you want to overwrite resources (since you are doing a fresh install, you can leave this blank, but if you've already imported this MSI and are doing it for a second time, select this option). Importing the tracking settings just means you'll keep any customizations to the default tracking that you may have had on ports, pipelines, or orchestrations.

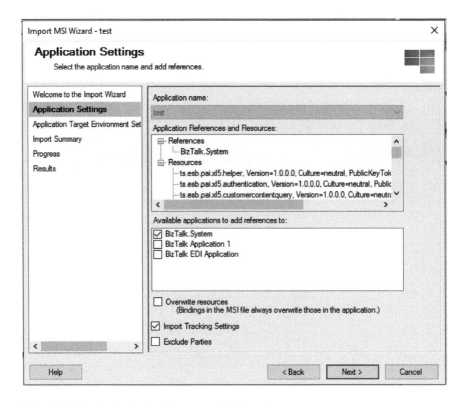

Figure 2.16: The Application Settings page of the import process

The MSI will now begin to import. If everything is in line, you will get a successful import, but it is common to get an error of some sort the first few times. Often, there are referenced DLLs that you have overlooked. For example, the error in Figure 2.17 says it is missing the Microsoft.Samples.BizTalk.XlangCustomFormatters assembly, which is a common assembly used for SMTP email formatting from orchestrations. In this case, the error can be resolved by canceling the MSI import, deploying this assembly manually (via the steps outlined earlier in this chapter on manual assembly deployment), and starting the MSI importer again.

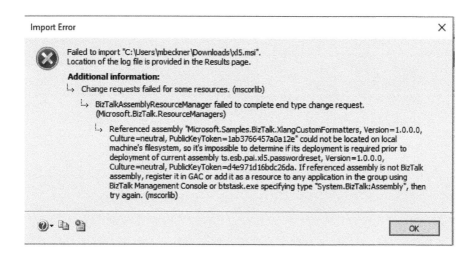

Figure 2.17: A missing assembly causes the importer to fail

It is not uncommon to have to try importing the MSI a number of times before it successfully imports, especially with solutions that have many artifacts. If you get errors that are difficult to address, try exporting smaller MSIs – or handling portions of the deployment manually.

When you get a successful import of the MSI, you still have two things to do. You must import the bindings in order to configure any ports or other BizTalk components, and you must register the assemblies into the GAC. You've looked at registering assemblies, and that is typically done after the binding import.

Importing the binding file can take some work. The steps are easy enough – right-click the application in the BizTalk 2016 Admin Console and select Import and then Bindings. The dialogue box shown in Figure 2.18 will be displayed. Browse to the file that you exported from your old version of BizTalk and click OK.

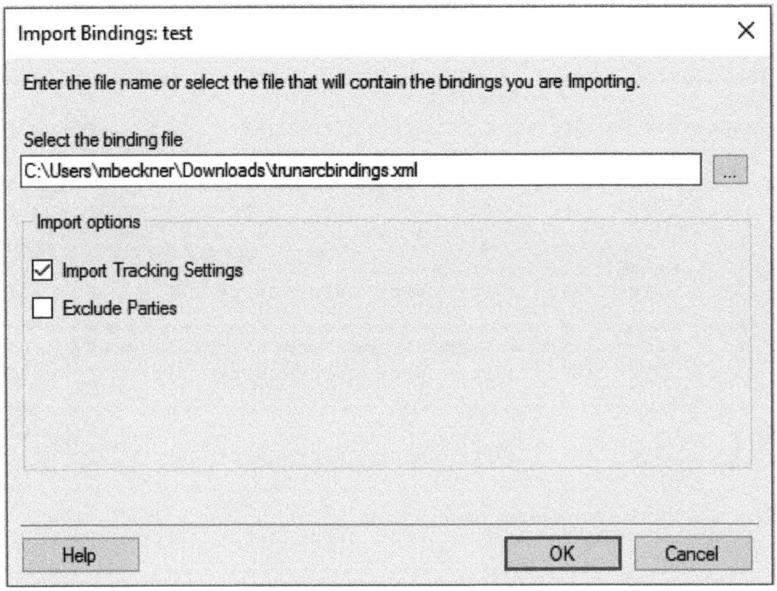

Figure 2.18: Importing the bindings file

Upon importing the bindings file, it is very likely that you will get an error. The binding import process requires that everything match exactly in the target environment to what was in the source. For example, if you have a local path where you were archiving files on your original server, and that path was C:\Archive, the binding import process will require that the same exact path exists on the new environment. If it does not, you will receive an error and must either create that directory and try importing the binding file again, or modify the binding file to alter the file path to a new path that exists on the new server.

Passwords may be converted to masked values (usually ******) when exported to binding files. If they are, you can either alter them in the binding file to their true values prior to importing, or you can change the value in the send or receive port configurations once the bindings have imported successfully. You will have passwords on ports that use FTP, SFTP, SQL, and other secure adapter types.

In the error shown in Figure 2.19, a pipeline assembly is missing in the target environment. The binding file is trying to set the Send Pipeline property on the Send Port, and is unable to find the missing assembly. In this case, the pipeline must first be deployed (either manually or via an MSI) before running the binding import process again.

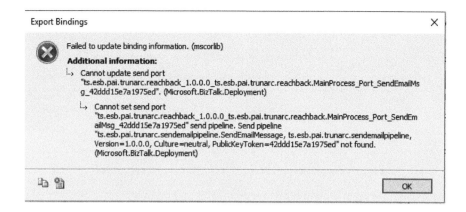

Figure 2.19: A missing assembly causes the bindings import to fail

You may need to modify the binding file manually to get certain properties to point to the correct things in your new 2016 environment. The file directory example just mentioned is common; most likely you would want to change the file path from a local directory to a network share. Other common changes would be FTP server URLs, usernames, SMTP addresses, and other values that would be different between environments. Altering the bindings file can be done in a text editor (such as notepad, shown in Figure 2.20).

Validating Your Deployment

Once you have everything deployed, you can begin testing your deployment. You'll want some sort of formal process here to make sure each component in your solution has been checked.

You'll begin by enabling ports and starting orchestrations. In the scenario from earlier in this chapter (the orchestration exposed as a web service) the receive port listens to inbound web requests to the proxy web service hosted in IIS. You will want to create a test harness (perhaps in a C# EXE that you write, or by using a third-party testing tool like SoapUI by SmartBear) to call the web service and begin testing your solution. As you test your newly deployed solution, you will want to check for errors that would indicate that something in the code will not run as expected in 2016. The easiest way is to monitor the Windows Event log on your 2016 environment and see what exceptions may be raised.

```
trunarcbindings - Notepad
File  Edit  Format  View  Help
    <ReceiveLocations>
      <ReceiveLocation Name="WebService_ts.esb.pai.trunarc.instrumentsyncquery_Proxy/ts_esb
        <Description xsi:nil="true" />
        <Address>/ts.esb.pai.trunarc.instrumentsyncquery_Proxy/ts_esb_pai_trunarc_instrumen
        <PublicAddress />
        <Primary>true</Primary>
        <ReceiveLocationServiceWindowEnabled>false</ReceiveLocationServiceWindowEnabled>
        <ReceiveLocationFromTime>2000-01-01T04:00:00</ReceiveLocationFromTime>
        <ReceiveLocationToTime>2000-01-01T03:59:59</ReceiveLocationToTime>
        <ReceiveLocationStartDateEnabled>false</ReceiveLocationStartDateEnabled>
        <ReceiveLocationStartDate>2011-10-21T00:00:00</ReceiveLocationStartDate>
        <ReceiveLocationEndDateEnabled>false</ReceiveLocationEndDateEnabled>
        <ReceiveLocationEndDate>2011-10-22T23:59:59</ReceiveLocationEndDate>
        <ReceiveLocationTransportType Name="SOAP" Capabilities="899" ConfigurationClsid="7e
        <ReceiveLocationTransportTypeData>&lt;CustomProps&gt;&lt;UseSSO vt="11"&gt;0&lt;/Us
        <ReceivePipeline Name="Microsoft.BizTalk.DefaultPipelines.XMLReceive" FullyQualifie
        <ReceivePipelineData xsi:nil="true" />
        <SendPipeline Name="Microsoft.BizTalk.DefaultPipelines.PassThruTransmit" FullyQuali
        <SendPipelineData xsi:nil="true" />
        <Enable>true</Enable>
        <ReceiveHandler Name="BizTalkServerIsolatedHost" HostTrusted="true">
          <TransportType Name="SOAP" Capabilities="899" ConfigurationClsid="7e104b2f-003c-4
        </ReceiveHandler>
      </ReceiveLocation>
    </ReceiveLocations>
    <SendPipelineData xsi:nil="true" />
```

Figure 2.20: You will frequently need to modify the binding file for it to import successfully

It is very possible that your code will migrate as-is. If it doesn't, then it will likely run but experience issues in mappings. Only by viewing the output of the full end-to-end process will you know if all your fields have mapped as you would expect. You will likely want to test each of your maps individually in Visual Studio 2015, using sample instances as the input to the maps, to make sure there are no errors. Errors and mapping inconsistencies can be masked when running in a deployed environment. See Chapter 3 for more detail on testing and upgrading maps.

Once you've determined if there are code changes that are required, you can decide if you want to do any of the following:

1. Do simple upgrades to the solution to make it more modern. For example, using the orchestration as a web service scenario, you may want to republish the orchestration as WCF service instead of SOAP. You can use the BizTalk WCF Service Publishing Wizard in this scenario, and immediately modernize your service without any code modifications.

2. Take steps to simplify your orchestrations or maps. This is your opportunity to make modifications that can make your code easier to work with. See Chapter 3 for ideas on how to do this.

Summary

This chapter has outlined how to deploy your solution to BizTalk Server 2016. Your goal should be to migrate the solution as-is as early in your project process as possible. From this exercise, you will quickly uncover several things:

1. The complexity of your solution. How many applications are you dealing with? How many BizTalk artifacts, individual assemblies, and manual configurations are you going to need? How much of the migration will need to be manual, versus how much can be done through MSIs and bindings?
2. How many non-BizTalk components are going to have to be migrated? There are frequently helper assemblies, custom databases, config file settings, web service proxies, and other components that are not directly part of the Biz-Talk engine, but that are very much part of your custom integration solution. These must be migrated separately.
3. How much of your code will you need to reorganize, update, or rewrite? If you find that your applications won't import because you are missing assemblies, or your maps don't work because the way they were written isn't compatible with BizTalk 2016, then you can begin to plan for the resourcing needed to handle a successful upgrade

Chapter 3
Visual Studio and Maps

As outlined in earlier chapters, you may have code that can be migrated without changes, or you may have to make alterations to components to get them to deploy properly. In cases where you must recompile (or want to in order to utilize the latest versions of .NET), you must upgrade your Visual Studio code base. This chapter will walk you through upgrading and recompiling your solutions, as well as testing and making modifications to your maps. You'll look at how to migrate a map from traditional functoids to XSLT, which is a vital skill to know for advanced mapping scenarios.

Recompiling Your Code in Visual Studio 2015

You've worked through migrating your components as-is from an older version of BizTalk to BizTalk 2016, as outlined in Chapter 2. Now, you will look at recompiling components before deployment. While you have seen that recompiling may not be necessary to move your BizTalk solutions from an older version of BizTalk to a new 2016 environment, there are many situations where recompiling your components will be necessary. These include:

1. You have all your source code, well organized, and available. Often, with legacy solutions, the original source code has been lost, and recompiling requires piecing together code from questionable sources. If your BizTalk solutions migrate "as is" and you do not have the source code, then your solutions may still function. If you have all your original source code, then recompiling everything before deployment using Visual Studio 2015 will ensure that your compiled code is up to date and running on the latest .NET framework.
2. You have components that do not migrate "as is," and therefore require code updates. These code updates must be done in Visual Studio 2015 and recompiled for deployment.
3. During your migration, you are adding new functionality to your processes or simplifying your architecture. Any required new component work will need to be done in Visual Studio 2015.

DOI 10.1515/9781501506086-003

As a developer, you may find some of this information to be very basic. Remember that the audience to a migration will often be someone who was not part of the original development of the
code and is new to BizTalk. In many of the organizations I have worked with, the people doing
the upgrade not only do not know BizTalk, they frequently have not worked with .NET. Having a
basic walk-through of working with Visual Studio is intended for this audience.

Let's begin by looking at upgrading an older version of a Visual Studio BizTalk
solution to Visual Studio 2015. The first step is to open Visual Studio 2015 and
select the project or solution you will be upgrading. As shown in Figure 3.1, you
can click on File on the toolbar and then select Open and Project/Solution. This
will allow you to browse to your file.

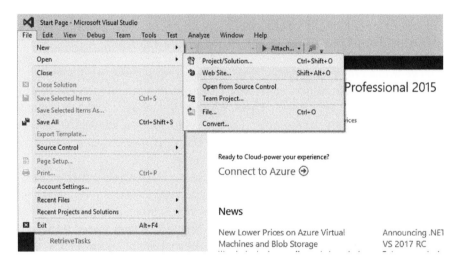

Figure 3.1: Open your project from within Visual Studio 2015

Figure 3.2 shows that the icon for the project is a Visual Studio 2010 project. You
will open this older file and Visual Studio will handle the upgrade.

Figure 3.2: File type icon shows Visual Studio 2010, which is the old source solution that will
upgrade

Once the solution opens, you will get a warning similar to what's shown in Figure 3.3. You can click OK – just make sure you have a backup of your code somewhere else in case you need to refer to something in the original code.

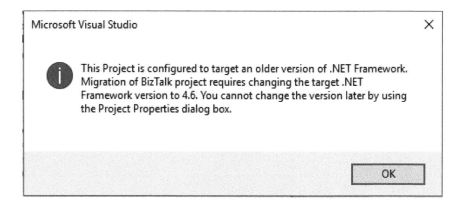

Figure 3.3: A pre-upgrade warning that can be ignored

After you click OK on the warning, Visual Studio will immediately begin to load the solution (see Figure 3.4). The warning will pop up for every project in the solution, unless you uncheck the "Ask me" option in the security warning dialog box.

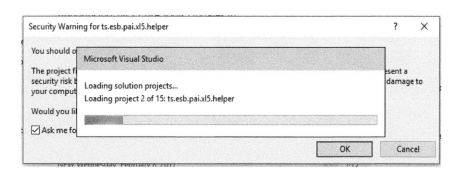

Figure 3.4: Security warning will pop up for each project in the solution as it loads

---

When your solution has fully loaded, you'll want to try to build it. You should get in the habit of selecting the "Rebuild" option (as shown in Figure 3.5), as this ensures that you are forcing a recompile of all projects (or projects referenced within a single project, if you are rebuilding at the Visual Studio project level). This can be done by right-clicking the solution, or any of the individual projects, and selecting Rebuild Solution.

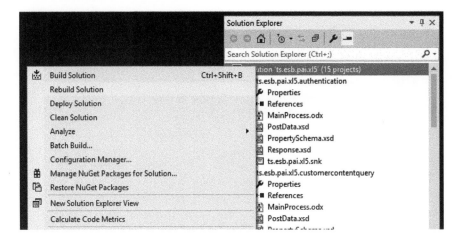

Figure 3.5: Rebuilding the projects in the solution

The solution used in this example and within the screenshots in this section has 15 projects associated with it. Upon rebuilding the code, we receive 14 errors, many of which are repeating (see Figure 3.6). In this case, the issue is that a referenced assembly is missing from a number of the projects. This assembly is used for email formatting in this solution, and is an assembly that was downloaded from somewhere on the internet many years ago.

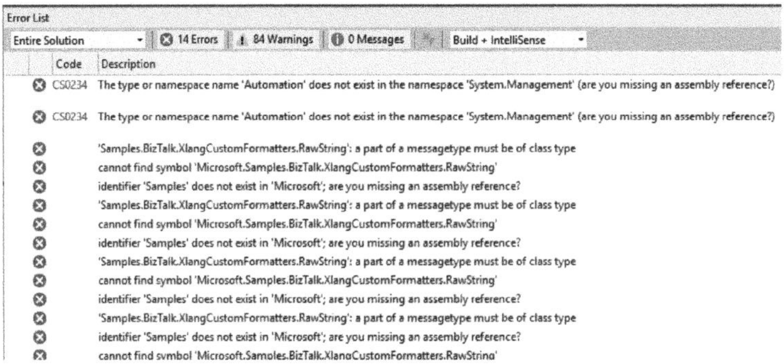

Figure 3.6: Errors after compiling

You can see in Figure 3.7 that the assembly in question still appears in the project References folder, but it can't be found. To resolve this error, right-click on
any of the projects that are missing the reference and browse to the assembly
(see Figure 3.8). Updating this in one of your projects should cause it to be updated in all your projects once you build the solution again.

Thankfully, in this case, I can go to my previous 2010 BizTalk Server and grab the missing assembly. However, you may have a case where you are missing an assembly or a project, and
can't rebuild your solution. Unfortunately, your options are limited. If you can grab the assembly
from the GAC on the old machine, then you may be able to migrate it "as-is." But, if it throws
errors, and you don't have the original code, you'll have to rewrite something!

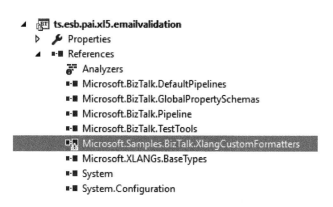

Figure 3.7: The assembly is missing in the project references

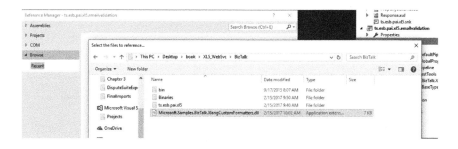

Figure 3.8: Browsing to a compiled version of the missing assembly fixes the missing references

With this assembly now referenced properly and a fresh rebuild of the solution,
there are now only two errors, both coming from a C# class library assembly.

This assembly is referenced within the projects from the various orchestrations, and is used to interact with a SQL server database. The code in this is pretty ancient, and there shouldn't be anything in it that doesn't migrate, but this error indicates that "Automation" does not exist in the System.Management reference (see Figure 3.9).

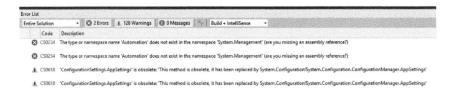

Figure 3.9: Two errors remain

Clicking on the .cs file within the class library project and scrolling to the top of the file causes this error to convert to a warning. The warning shows that the "automation" assembly reference resulted from a change in the .NET framework. The other warnings indicate that a call used to pull configurable fields from the BizTalk configuration file has been deprecated but, in this case, is still completely functional and valid. At this point, the errors are all resolved and the solution completes the recompiling of all the assemblies (Figure 3.10).

After the Visual Studio code upgrade process, there often are temporary errors the compiler has to work with that will automatically resolve on their own. If you run into issues that make no sense, try closing out of Visual Studio and reopening the project files. This frequently will resolve issues as well.

Figure 3.10: All that are left are warnings

In this example, no further code changes are required to get the code to compile. This does not mean, however, that the maps and orchestrations will work exactly as they are supposed to. All components must be deployed and tested to validate that they function as they should.

With solutions that contain multiple projects (which virtually every well-organized BizTalk solution should have), you can save time by compiling your DLLs to a single file directory. The default is to have these compile within a subfolder of each directory, which means that in order to deploy you must browse to a different directory for each assembly. Instead, you should modify the default output path on the project properties to a single top level directory where all assemblies can be written to. Figure 3.11 shows the project property settings and a relative path in the Output path. This path is defined as .\..\Binaries, and this can be used in every project to push to a top-level folder called Binaries.

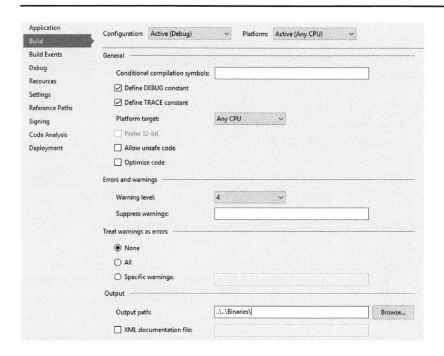

Figure 3.11: Set the compiled assembly Output path property to a common directory for all projects

Restructuring Your Code in Visual Studio 2015

As mentioned in Chapter 1, you need to work to always ensure you have small projects that compile down into unique aspects of work. For example, the project shown in Figure 3.12 has many maps in a single project. This compiles into a single DLL and can be both resource intensive and difficult to maintain and update.

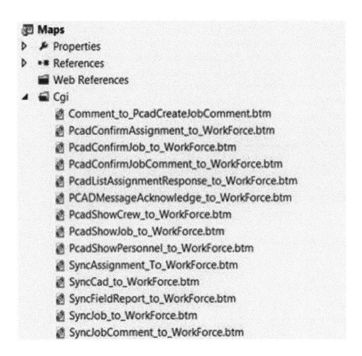

Figure 3.12: Avoid creating a project that has many BizTalk artifacts in it

The developer who created this apparently decided to organize the BizTalk solution so that a single project had all the maps for the various pieces of work. What happens here is that all these maps compile to a single assembly. That means several things:

1. Any time one of these maps is called, the whole assembly must instantiate, requiring more system resources than if the map were compiled into its own separate assembly.

2. Any time an update to one map is needed, all the maps must be recompiled and redeployed. This makes any production deployment substantially more difficult and often means having to stop production processes while the deployment takes place. If the map was compiled into a single assembly, it could be deployed in a few seconds with only a restart of the BizTalk host required.

3. The map project is referenced by a variety of projects, which means any time a build occurs, all of these must be rebuilt.

The correct architecture here is to split these maps into individual projects (and therefore assemblies, since every project builds to its own .NET assembly). In most cases, that means one map per project. In cases where multiple maps may be chained together within a single process, these maps would reside in a single project. Your goal should be to have as few artifacts in each project as possible and to split these out into as many individual project as you can.

In this restructuring, you will also want to be smart about how you name your projects. Using namespacing allows for ease of organization as well as naming. I will typically name a solution CompanyName.BizTalk, and then add projects to that solution that look like CompanyName.BizTalk.ProjectName.TypeOfProject. In practice, this looks like what is shown in Figure 3.13. On the left is a solution with projects split out by component type, while on the right the solution's projects are split out by the type of work the project is doing. In both cases, I can keep the unique pieces of code separate from one another to ensure I have an easy way to deploy my code.

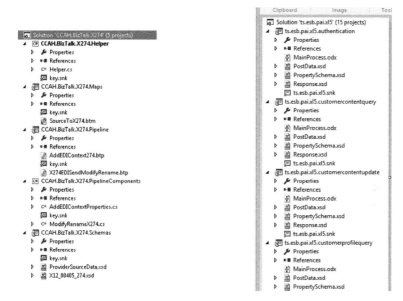

Figure 3.13: Splitting out the project structure – two examples of patterns for this

Testing Upgraded Maps

There are two ways to test maps. The first is from within Visual Studio, the second after deployment in a working scenario. To test from Visual Studio, you must have a valid instance for the source data. In some solutions, this will be easy to come by – in others, especially where multiple maps are used in succession within an orchestration – it may be more challenging. The easiest way to test is usually within Visual Studio, as it allows you to immediately see whether your code will still work in this upgraded version. In order to test your map in Visual Studio, take these steps:

1. Every map has a source and a target schema. You will need a valid XML or flat file instance for the source. Ideally, you have an archive of these documents you can pull from your old production BizTalk environment. If not, you may have to do some work to find an instance. This could include adding logging to your current production BizTalk system (that you are upgrading from) so that you can capture an XML document that matches the source schema to your map.
2. Right-click the map and select Properties.
3. For the TestMap Input property, set this to XML (or native if you are working with a flat file).
4. For the TestMap Input Instance property, browse to the XML instance you have from Step 1.
5. Set both the Validate TestMap properties to False; there is no need to validate the input or output now.
6. Right-click the map again and this time select Test Map. This will give you any errors that may have occurred. If no errors occur, this will give you the output XML file. You can view this output by holding Ctrl and clicking on it.

Look at the output that was created and compare it against a document of the same type in your current production system. This should tell you whether any discrepancies exist. Pay close attention to the output of any C# Script functoids, custom functoids, database lookups, or other complex functoids. These are prone to issues post-migration, and may have unexpected output that needs to be addressed through mapping updates.

Making Code Changes to Maps

You may find that your maps do not function as you would expect when you test them. Or you may find that the maps are so complex that they are virtually impossible to work through and make modifications to. If you are forced to make code changes to your maps, you will want to take the opportunity to rethink how your maps are programmed. Instead of using traditional functoids and relying on the mapping user interface, now is the time to look at XSLT as an option. XSLT is a powerful, versatile, and easy-to-learn language.

XSLT is essential to the successful development of advanced maps.

A map can consist of Inline XSLT, which allows you to combine standard functoids with XSLT script, or it can be entirely XSLT-based, and can reference an external XSLT style sheet. We'll look at examples from the first, as it is the most versatile and the one you'll want to incorporate into your mappings. The second can be done by setting the Custom XSLT Path property on your map – just click on the map surface, and you'll see the property (Figure 3.14). You can browse to an XSL sheet that you have developed externally.

Note that there is a new property in BizTalk 2016 called "Use XSL Transform." This was first released in a cumulative update for BizTalk 2013 R2. The way maps are compiled was changed in that version of BizTalk, and in doing so caused some mappings to no longer work as expected. One example was Boolean values used in Inline C# Script functoids. This property will allow you to override the new compiler and force BizTalk to compile your maps the way they were historically. If you see issues in the way Booleans are handled or other anomalies during your testing of BizTalk, you should try swapping this field to True or to False (default value is Undefined) and retesting. Doing so may save you some extensive debugging.

The way BizTalk maps are compiled by the Visual Studio compiler engine is different in BizTalk 2016 than in most previous version of BizTalk. You may need to experiment with the Use XSL Transform property in your map for certain code in functoids to work properly.

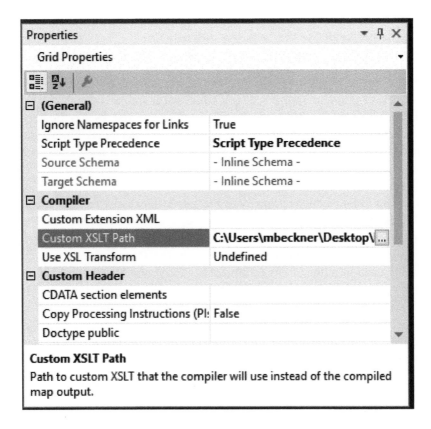

Figure 3.14: The XSLT properties for a map

Inline XSLT Basics

Inline XSLT is the most versatile code option you have within the mapper. Drop a Scripting functoid on the map surface, right-click it, and select Configuring Scripting Functoid. You can select either the "Inline XSLT" or the "Inline XSLT Call Template" option from the drop-down menu, as shown in Figure 3.15. The primary difference between these two is that with "Call Template" you can pass in parameters to your XSLT script, while you cannot do so with the other option. An example of passing parameters into an XSLT template is shown later in this chapter.

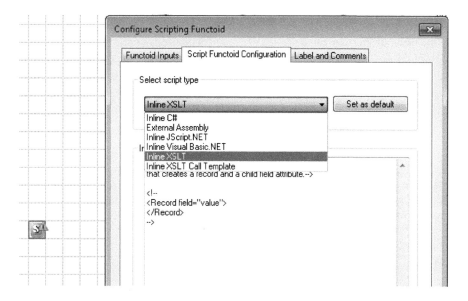

Figure 3.15: Selecting Inline XSLT as the functoid script type

When you first select the Inline XSLT option, it will give you a simple script that has been commented out. To get your bearings, remove the comments so that your script is just the <Record field="value"></Record> statement. Then, connect the output of your Scripting functoid to the root of your target schema (see Figure 3.16).

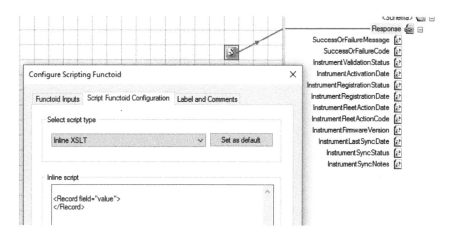

Figure 3.16: Using a basic Inline XSLT script

Next, you will want to test this and see what it produces. Right-click on the map and select properties. Set both the Validate TestMap Input and Validate TestMap Output properties to False. Setting these will free you up so that the Visual Studio tester isn't concerned about the structure of your testing inputs and outputs. The TestMap Input property for now can be left to Generate Instance, but if you have a valid XML instance to use as your source, it would be great to set this property to that file now. Figure 3.17 shows all these properties for reference.

During development of your maps, you will want to set the Validate TestMap Input and Validate Test Map Output properties to False. Once your maps are complete and you are producing the output you want, you may want to re-enable these flags. You'll then be able to fine-tune the output so that it matches what the schema is expecting.

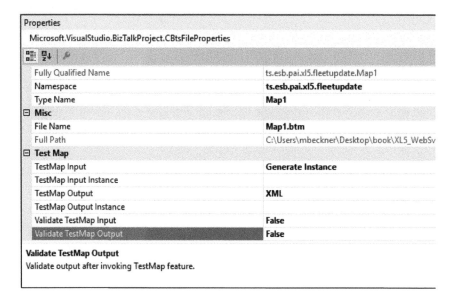

Figure 3.17: Test Map properties

You can now right-click your map file and select Test Map (as shown in Figure 3.18). In the Output window of Visual Studio, you will see a link next to "The output is stored in the following file." Hold down the Ctrl key on your keyboard and click this link. It will open the output, which will look like what you see in Figure 3.19.

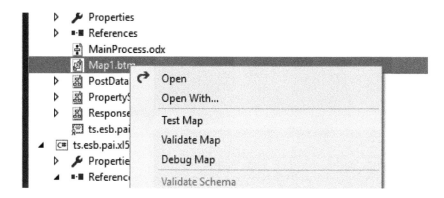

Figure 3.18: Testing the XSLT

Figure 3.19: The output of the Inline XSLT

As you can see, the Record node is placed at the root level of the document. This is because the output of the XSLT Inline script is pointed to the root node. Now, move the output of the functoid to one of the child nodes in the target schema, as shown in Figure 3.20.

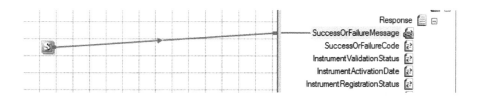

Figure 3.20: Moving the output of the Script functoid to a child node

Testing this will place the Record node that is in the XSLT script as a child node of the Response node – even though the schema itself has no element named Record. You can force any sort of structure or standard into the target document. Figure 3.21 shows this.

Figure 3.21: The output now is under the root node of the target document

Now, looking back at the script, alter it to give the name of the target node. In this case, the target that we are mapping to is called <SuccessOrFailureCode>, so the XSLT will change accordingly (as shown in Figure 3.22). In this example, we've added a value of SUCCESS (HARD CODE) as a hard-coded value in the script. The output of this is shown in Figure 3.23.

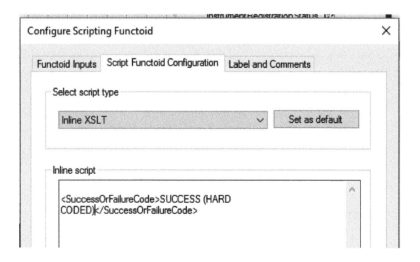

Figure 3.22: Setting the name of the written element to match the target schema

In many cases, your target schema and output XML instance will contain namespace prefixes at some of the element names. To find out if your situation will require them, right-click your target schema and generate a sample output XML instance. If this shows ns0 (or similar) in front of element names, then you will need to add these prefixes into your XSLT code. This can be done by typing them directly into the node name, such as <ns0:SuccessOrFailureCode>SUC-CESS</ns0:SuccessOrFailureCode>.

Figure 3.23: The output after hard-coding the value in the XSLT

Finally, we'll make the value in the output dynamic. This is done by pointing the XSLT script to a location in the source data where the data will be pulled from. There are many ways to traverse the source XML document. An example of a source schema is shown in Figure 3.24, while the XSLT updated mapping is shown in Figure 3.25. In this example, the script is going to look for the first occurrence at any location within the XML document of the ActionCode node. Using the dynamic script will cause the value in the source to be placed in the target node, as shown in Figure 3.26.

```
<?xml version="1.0"?>
<ns0:PostData xmlns:ns0="http://ts.esb.pai.xl5.fleetupdate.PostData">
    <SupportKey>SupportKey_0</SupportKey>
    <CustomerID>CustomerID_0</CustomerID>
    <Mode>Test</Mode>
    <VersionNumber>VersionNumber_0</VersionNumber>
    <Source>Source_0</Source>
    <Culture>Culture_0</Culture>
    <SerialNumber>SerialNumber_0</SerialNumber>
    <ActivationID>ActivationID_0</ActivationID>
    <InstrumentApplication>InstrumentApplication_0</InstrumentApplication>
    <InstrumentPrimaryUse>InstrumentPrimaryUse_0</InstrumentPrimaryUse>
    <ActionCode>A</ActionCode>
</ns0:PostData>
```

Figure 3.24: An example of the source XML document; ActionCode has a value of "A"

Figure 3.25: The XSLT now looks at the source XML for its data

Figure 3.26: The value from the source ActionCode is placed in the target SuccessOrFailureCode

The source schema is very simple, and this node occurs only once, so there are variety of ways to get at the data, including:

1. <xsl:value-of select="//ActionCode"/>. Finds the node anywhere within the source document.

2. <xsl:value-of select="/*/ActionCode"/>. Looks for ActionCode at the second level under the first node in the document.
3. <xsl:value-of select="//*/ActionCode"/>. Looks for ActionCode at the second level under the any node in the document.
4. <xsl:value-of select="/*[local-name()='PostData']ActionCode"/>. Looks for ActionCode under the PostData element in the source. The use of local-name() is required in this case, because the PostData node has a namespace prefix. Referring to it simply as //PostData does not work, as there is no element which matches that name exactly.
5. <xsl:value-of select="//ActionCode[1]"/>. This selects the first instance of the element that matches the XSLT. In the example we are using, there is only one ActionCode, so there is no need to declare this. In many cases, however, you will be working with more complex XML schemas, and there will be looping and recurring nodes. You may need to look at a specific instance of a value, and this allows you to access it much as you would an array in C# or other languages.

Most of the work in XSLT is experimentation. It can be tricky to get the logic correct at times, but it is a very simple language to learn, and one that you can figure out in an hour or two. Incorporating this into your maps is a must, and there is no better time than when you are forced to upgrade a map to add it in.

Passing Input Parameters to XSLT

You just looked at the basics of inline XSLT programming. The other option within the Scripting functoid is the XSLT Call Template. This acts the same as straight inline XSLT programming, except that you have the ability to pass input parameters into the code. Input parameters will work exactly as they would if you were passing them into a C# Script functoid. Figure 3.27 shows an example of passing in two input parameters from the source document you just looked at earlier.

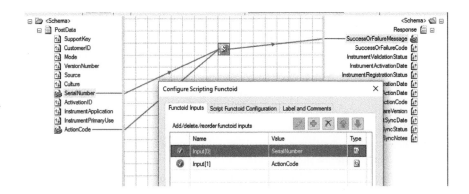

Figure 3.27: Passing in two input parameters to an Inline XSLT Call Template Script functoid

In the script (shown in Figure 3.28), there are two input parameters declared. These are declared in the same order that the inputs in the mapping interface are placed (SerialNumber is first, ActionCode is second). These parameters can be named anything you would like; they do not need to match the source node values. In this example script, these two parameters are used to create a simple output message, which will be placed inside of the SuccessOrFailureMessage node.

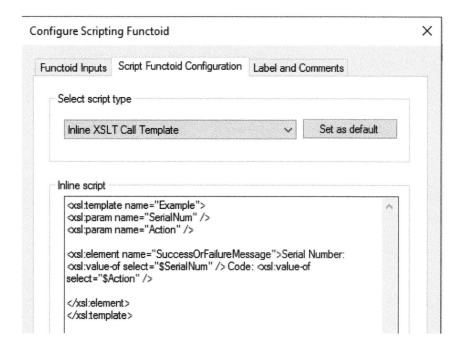

Figure 3.28: The Call Template script

The output is shown in Figure 3.29.

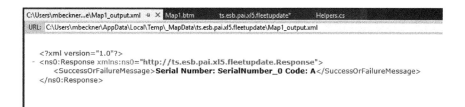

Figure 3.29: The concatenated output

Calling .NET Assemblies from XSLT

XSLT is a scripting language and has limitations for what can be done within it. In cases where you need to have complex logic – such as looking up data from a database or calling a web service – you will need to shell out to another component to do the work. Within the BizTalk map, you can allow your XSLT to call an external .NET assembly with relative ease.

Let's assume you have a C# class library function ready to be called. You've tested this function and are able to call it from a Windows test application or other C# component. Now, you want to call it from XSLT. You must begin by creating an XML file that can be used to reference the assembly from within your map. The following XML document is an example of referencing an existing assembly. Notice that it contains both the AssemblyName (including the PublicKey) and the ClassName (this is the class where the function you will be calling is contained).

```
<ExtensionObjects>
 < ExtensionObject
      Namespace="http://schemas.microsoft.com/Biz-
Talk/2003/ScriptNS0"
      AssemblyName="Sample.Helpers,version-1.0.0.0,Cul-
ture=neutral,PublicKey=fc0ed490c852c5c7"
      ClassName="Sample.Helpers.Helper"/>
</ExtensionObjects>
```

Save this XML document. It should be saved in the same place as your map file for ease of tracking. Once it is saved, reference it from the map property called Custom Extension XML, as shown in Figure 3.30.

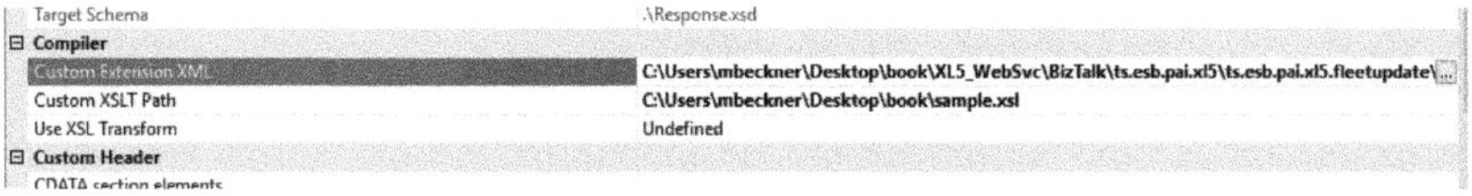

Figure 3.30: Referencing the Extension XML file you just created

Now, from within your XSLT code, you can call this method. If you were to call it from within the Call Template code you used earlier, it would look something like what is shown in Figure 3.31. The name of the function is Concatenate Data, and it takes two input parameters.

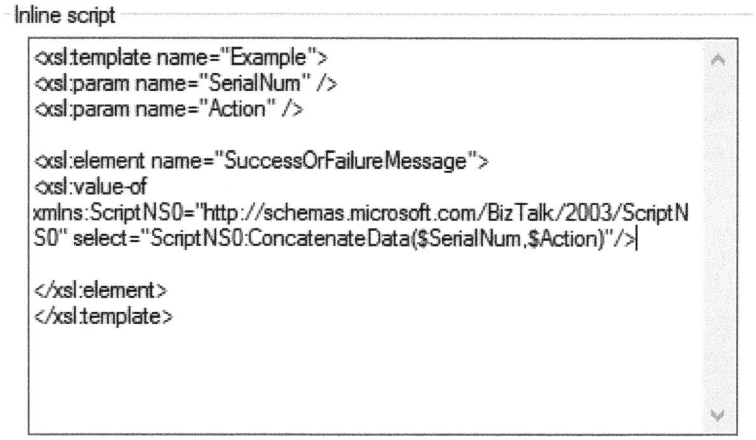

Inline script

```
<xsl:template name="Example">
<xsl:param name="SerialNum" />
<xsl:param name="Action" />

<xsl:element name="SuccessOrFailureMessage">
<xsl:value-of
xmlns:ScriptNS0="http://schemas.microsoft.com/BizTalk/2003/ScriptN
S0" select="ScriptNS0:ConcatenateData($SerialNum,$Action)"/>

</xsl:element>
</xsl:template>
```

Figure 3.31: Calling the assembly from within the XSLT script

You will need to make a manual modification to the .BTM map file. Outside of Visual Studio, from the file directory, right-click the BTM file and open it using notepad or similar text editor. Search for <TreeValues>. You will need to add a node right before this TreeValues node and right after the ScriptTypePreference node that precedes it. Your entry should look like the following:

```
<CustomXSLT XsltPath="" ExtObjXmlPath="[Path to your XML
File]"/>
```

Adding it between the two existing nodes in the BTM file looks like this:

```
</ScriptTypePreferences><CustomXSLT XsltPath="" Ex-
tObjXmlPath="Extension.XML"/><TreeValues>
```

After adding the CustomXSLT extension via the text editor to your BTM file, it may be lost if you load the file again from Visual Studio. You will want to have the map already loaded in Visual Studio, and make the save in the text editor outside of Visual Studio. Make sure and add it back in if it gets lost.

After doing this, you will be able to call the assembly from your XSLT within your map. You are also able to debug your .NET assembly from the map by taking these steps:

1. Deploy your referenced C# assembly to the GAC.
2. Have your map open in Visual Studio.
3. In a separate instance of Visual Studio, open your C# library project that you used to compile the assembly that was deployed in Step 1.
4. In this second Visual Studio instance (C#), place a breakpoint on the function that your XSLT is calling.
5. Click the Debug option from the menu in the second instance of Visual Studio and select Attach. Select the devenv.exe that maps to your first Visual Studio instance. This will cause this code in the second Visual Studio instance to kick off when the assembly that is in the GAC is called from the context of the first Visual Studio instance.
6. Test your map in your first Visual Studio instance. This should cause the breakpoint to be hit when the XSLT calls it.

Summary

You've looked at recompiling your code in Visual Studio 2015 and at restructuring your Visual Studio projects so that they are easier to compile. You've also looked at testing maps and revising your maps to use XSLT. XSLT is your most powerful tool within the BizTalk mapping environment. Take time to learn it, whether you include it in revised maps required by your migration or just in new maps that you develop in the future. Chapter 4 will look at upgrading orchestrations and external components that may be used by those orchestrations or by maps.

Chapter 4
Orchestrations and C#

When it comes to compilation, your orchestrations most likely will upgrade exactly as they were written in previous versions of BizTalk (unless they are older than BizTalk 2006, in which case you will likely need to rewrite everything from scratch). However, even though the processes may compile without rewrite, the orchestrations may be overly complex, and the architecture used may be outdated and in need of simplification. You should put some thought into how you might rearchitect your orchestrations. This chapter will outline some common approaches to orchestration development that lead to complex solutions that should be rethought prior to upgrading. Alternative approaches to these complex architectures are outlined.

Revisiting SQL Server Integrations

There are a number of ways to call SQL Server from a BizTalk orchestration. The most common is to use the adapters and ports within orchestrations to import the schemas and interact with the database directly. There are some very advanced wizards and tools within BizTalk that allow for this. In this section, we'll compare this approach with calling the database through a data access layer using a C# class library. The goal is to demonstrate that you can greatly simplify your orchestrations by using C# in comparison to using the out-of-the-box modeling BizTalk provides.

Integrating C# classes into your orchestrations can greatly reduce complexity and improve development time.

For this example, we'll look at an orchestration that makes several calls to a database. Each interaction with the database requires a Send and Receive shape within the orchestration. As shown in Figure 4.1, a message is constructed and then sent to the database, while the response is posted back to the orchestration. In this image, there are two calls to the database.

DOI 10.1515/9781501506086-004

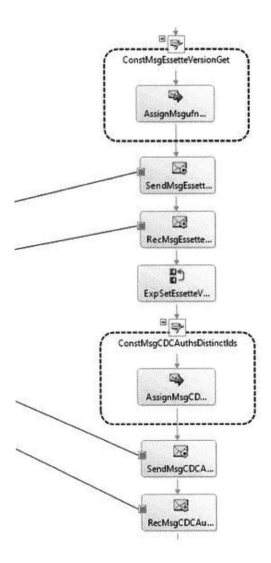

Figure 4.1: An orchestration calling SQL through traditional ports

Using any of the SQL adapters will automatically generate schemas that represent the input and output of the calls to the database. These schemas can become very sizable, and are not always accurate or exactly what you may want brought back from the database. They are also weighty and can become very cumbersome to work with. Take a look at Figure 4.2 – the names generated can be difficult to follow and can represent different sets of data that may be returned.

Figure 4.2: Schema elements auto-generated can be weighty and difficult to work with

In a scenario where there will be many calls to and from a database, the complexity of the process can increase exponentially. In the example in Figure 4.3, the orchestration initiates, makes a decision based on a value passed into it, and then calls the database with different parameters. As you may be able to see, there are 10 calls to the database. The zoom has to be set at 30% to fit all the flow into a single window.

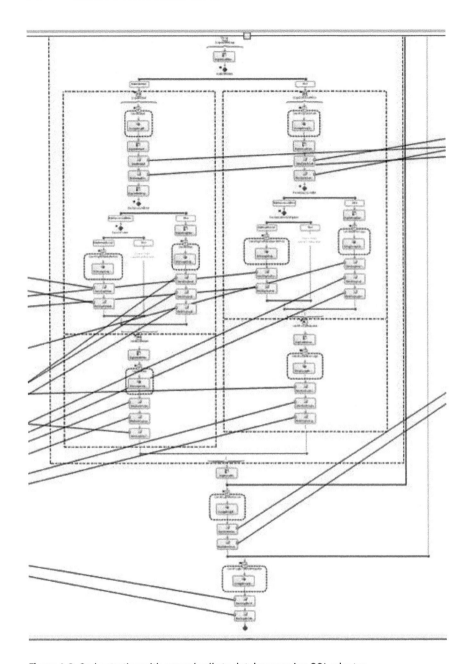

Figure 4.3: Orchestration with several calls to databases using SQL adapter

Each of the calls in this orchestration requires a separate input and output schema. The number of schemas becomes overwhelming, as you can see in Figure 4.4. And, in order to use these schemas within an orchestration, all the messages in Figure 4.5 and all the ports in Figure 4.6 must be created and utilized. If you were to build in maps for each of these calls, you can see that your process becomes increasing unsupportable. Even if this can be developed and tested by the first BizTalk developer, it will:

— Take an extremely long time to develop, compared with other methods
— Be difficult for the original developer to maintain and support
— Will be difficult to transfer to another developer in the future
— Will be complex and time consuming to test and validate

Figure 4.4: Many schemas are required for multiple calls to the database within one orchestration

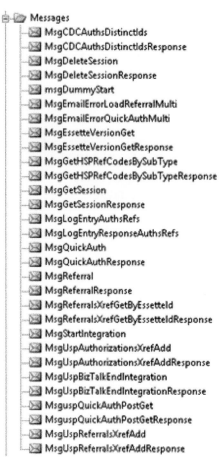

Figure 4.5: Every schema must map to a message to be used in an orchestration

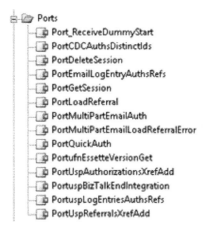

Figure 4.6: Many ports must be configured within the orchestration to handle the SQL communications

Simplifying SQL Server Integrations

There is no doubt that using the out-of-the-box approach to integrating with SQL Server creates BizTalk solutions that are complex, and in many cases so complex they are unsupportable and extremely difficult to migrate and upgrade. What can be done to change this? There is a very straightforward and simple way to interact with SQL that does not require schemas. This approach uses C# and referenced classes within BizTalk orchestrations. This can allow for the following:

1. Complete control over your code, without the use of wizards that auto-generate components.
2. Processes that can be tested outside of BizTalk before incorporating them into an orchestration.
3. Reduced development time.
4. Simplified flows and code.

To illustrate this approach, we'll first look at calling a stored procedure that has one input parameters and one output parameter. The orchestration will call the stored procedure via a C# function. The flow of this communication pattern is shown in Figure 4.7.

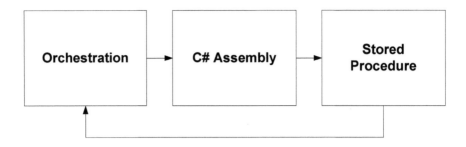

Figure 4.7: Example scenario uses this pattern to communicate with the database

Generally, you will want to start development with the stored procedure, as this will allow you to ensure your database level functions are working as expected before ever trying to call from BizTalk. In this case, the stored procedure takes the two input parameters and does a lookup against a database table. This lookup will be used to populate the output parameter. Listing 4.1 shows a simple stored procedure that performs this functionality.

Listing 4.1. Stored Procedure

```
CREATE PROCEDURE [dbo].[CustomerLookup]
   @emailAddress          NVARCHAR(255),
   @customerID            VARCHAR(50) OUTPUT
AS
BEGIN

  SET NOCOUNT ON

  SELECT @customerID = CustomerID
  FROM GlobalCustomerRegistration
  WHERE EmailAddress = @emailAddress

END
```

This stored procedure should be tested prior to integrating with any other components. It can be tested using the code shown in Listing 4.2. Typically, this sample code should be added to the comments of the stored procedure so that it can be easily referenced and reused in the future. For procedures more complex than this one, you will need to call the code multiple times as you develop it, and it is helpful to have the execution code available in the comments of the stored procedure itself.

Listing 4.2. Calling the Stored Procedure

```
/*****
 Usage:
 DECLARE @emailAddress nvarchar(255)
 ,@customerID varchar(50)
 SET @emailAddress = 'mdbeckner@hotmail.com'

 EXEC CustomerLookup @emailAddress,@customerID OUTPUT

 SELECT @customerID
*****/
```

With the stored procedure developed and tested, you can now create the .NET assembly and function that will call it. You should add a C# class library project to the same solution where your orchestration is located for easy reference. This class library will compile into an assembly (DLL) that will need to be deployed to the Global Assembly Cache once it has been completed.

You should come up with a common naming pattern for assemblies that are called from your orchestration, and that are used exclusively by your BizTalk components. For this example, they are named with the same namespace as the main orchestration and schema projects and include the name of "helper" in the project name, as shown in Figure 4.8.

Figure 4.8: A C# Class Library can be added to your BizTalk solution

The code in Listing 4.3 shows the C# used to call the stored procedure that was put together earlier. This code includes all of the class declaration as well as the function call itself.

Always mark your class as [Serializable], as shown directly after the namespace declaration in the code shown in Listing 4.3. This allows you to call it from anywhere within your orchestration. If you do not mark it as [Serializable], you will have to wrap it in a transaction, which adds weight and complexity to your orchestration code.

Listing 4.3. C# Class and Function

```csharp
using System;
using System.Collections.Generic;
using System.Linq;
using System.Text;
using System.Xml;
using System.Data.SqlClient;
using System.Data;
using System.IO;
using System.Management.Automation;
using System.Management.Automation.Runspaces;
using System.Collections.ObjectModel;

namespace ts.esb.pai.xl5.helper
{
  [Serializable]
  public class Helpers
  {
    public void CallSprocOne(string strEmailAddress, out string
    strCustomerID, string strConnectionString)
{
  string strStoredProcedure = "CustomerLookup";

  using (SqlConnection Connection = new SqlConnection(strConnectionString))
    {
    SqlCommand Command = new SqlCommand(strStoredProcedure, Connection);

    Command.CommandType = CommandType.StoredProcedure;

    SqlParameter ParameterEmailAddress = new SqlParameter("@emailAddress",
    strEmailAddress);

    Command.Parameters.Add(ParameterEmailAddress);

    SqlParameter ParameterCustomerID = new SqlParameter("@customerID",
    SqlDbType.VarChar, 50);
```

```
    ParameterCustomerID.Direction = ParameterDirection.Out-
put;

    Command.Parameters.Add(ParameterCustomerID);

    Connection.Open();

    SqlDataReader Reader = Command.ExecuteReader();

    strCustomerID = Command.Parameters["@custom-
erID"].Value.ToString();
    strRegistrationState =

    Command.Parameters["@registration-
State"].Value.ToString();

    Connection.Close();
   }
  }
 }
```

You can test the assembly before you ever integrate it into BizTalk by creating a Windows Form application or other EXE that can be used as a test harness. Working to eliminate errors and simplify your flow is your goal in everything you are doing with a rewrite, so ensuring that your C# works the way you would expect before adding it to the orchestration flow is good practice. When you have the C# ready, you will need to add a reference to it in the References folder of your Biz-Talk project that holds the orchestration (see Figure 4.9).

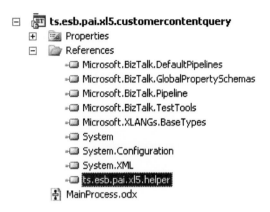

Figure 4.9: Referencing the helper class in your BizTalk orchestration project

After the reference has been made, you'll be able to call the C# function from an Expression shape within the BizTalk orchestration. The code within the Expression shape contains the call into the function. You'll first need to determine where the data will come from. Let's assume the two input values come from promoted properties on the input schema. Figure 4.10 shows a schema with its elements promoted as Distinguished Fields, which allow for these fields to be easily referenced within an orchestration.

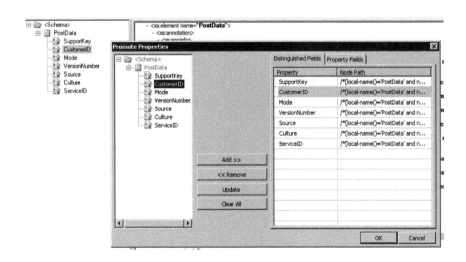

Figure 4.10: Promoted properties on a schema

The output parameter from the stored procedure will need to be placed into an orchestration variable. This can be done in Visual Studio by opening the orchestration, clicking on the Orchestration View tab, and creating a new Variable (as shown in Figure 4.11). The variable type should match the type being returned from the database – in this case, the output is a varchar, so the variable should be of type System.String.

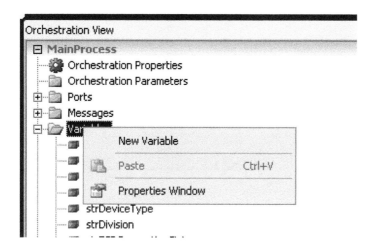

Figure 4.11: Create a new variable to hold the value of the output parameter from the stored procedure

In addition to defining the string variable, you will also need to create a variable that can be used as an instance of the C# class. This can be done by creating a new variable, and selecting ".NET Class" as the Type property, as shown in Figure 4.12. This will open a dialogue box (Figure 4.13) where you will be able to browse to the appropriate class (this can be done only if the class library has been referenced in the Visual Studio Project References folder).

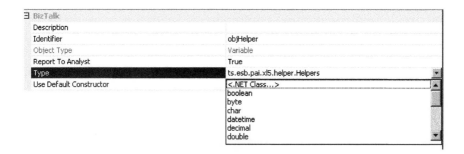

Figure 4.12: Selecting a .NET Class as the Type property

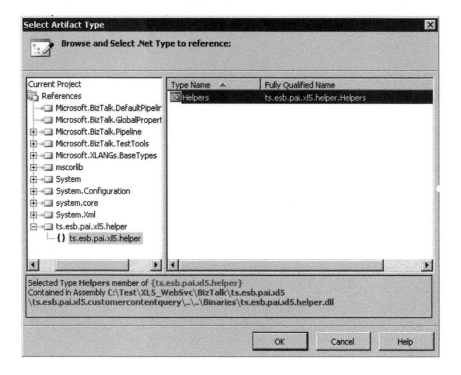

Figure 4.13: Browsing to the referenced class

With the inputs to the stored procedure coming from the input schema, and the output of the stored procedure being placed into a newly defined variable, you can now create an Expression shape and add a single line of code to it. This code will call the C# function, which will in turn call the database. An example of calling the CallSprocOne function defined in Listing 4.3 above is shown below. Note that the strCustomerID property has an "out" directive before it, which will ensure the field gets populated and can be used later in the stored procedure (most likely as an input to another call to a database).

```
objHelper.CallSprocOne(msgPostData.EmailAddress,out
strCustomerID,strConnString);
```

With everything completed, the call to the stored procedure will use a single Expression shape within the orchestration, with no input or output ports required. If all that was being done in the orchestration was the initial instantiation based on the input message and the call to the database, then the orchestration could be fully functional, communicating with a database, with only two shapes and one line of code, as shown in Figure 4.14.

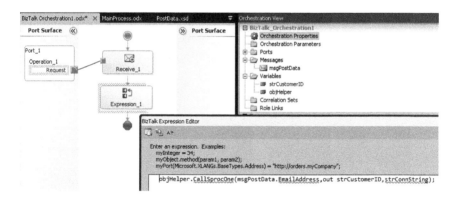

Figure 4.14: The remodeled orchestration

The level of effort to develop, test, deploy, and maintain an orchestration like this is exponentially lower than the amount of work required to deal with the traditional SQL adapter port approach. The amount of flexibility and control you have over the code is also far greater. Instead of being held at the mercy of wizards and auto-generated schemas, you can build highly efficient components that rely on good coding practices.

SQL and XML

An advanced way to interact with the database is to pass in a full XML document to a stored procedure, and let the stored procedure parse through the data and insert it into the database. This eliminates any of the data manipulation from the BizTalk components and moves it over almost entirely to SQL Server. Often, you can eliminate maps altogether and process your data at its most native level. This is often most valuable with complex schemas and database heavy integrations. EDI solutions are a great example.

To illustrate how this works, we'll look at receiving an 837 EDI claims document. As Figure 4.15 shows, this will come in as a flat file, get converted by Biz-Talk into XML, the XML will be picked up by an orchestration and then sent to a stored procedure. The stored procedure will use XQuery to parse out the data and insert it into tables.

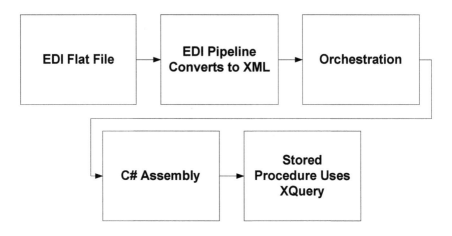

Figure 4.15: Example scenario receives an EDI flat file and lets the stored procedure parse the resulting XML

Moving data manipulation and logic to the database component tier, rather than leaving it within BizTalk, can greatly simplify your code. It can also make it maintainable by a far larger number of developers. There are many more people who can revise a SQL stored procedure than can revise a BizTalk orchestration.

An 837 document has a tremendous amount of data in it, with repeating nodes at numerous levels within the document. Let's look specifically at the CLM (claim)

level of the document. This data, in its converted XML format, will be sent into the stored procedure shown in Listing 4.4. The stored procedure will look for all occurrences of the CLM information at the level defined in the CROSS APPLY notations. It will get every instance of it and insert three pieces of information into a row in a table for every occurrence.

Listing 4.4. Using XQuery to parse an 837 EDI XML Document

```
CREATE PROCEDURE [dbo].[spInsertInboundData837]
 @vchSourceFileName As varchar(500)
 ,@vchTradingPartner As varchar(50)
 ,@xmlSourceData As XML
AS
BEGIN
SET NOCOUNT ON;

-- the following will remove namespace declarations for ease
of parsing
SELECT      CAST(REPLACE(CAST(@xmlSourceData      as      VAR-
CHAR(Max)),'ns0:','')AS XML) AS SOURCEDATA into #xml

INSERT INTO ClaimTable
-- this will get the CLM data at the subscriber level
SELECT
 pc.value('CLM01_PatientControlNumber[1]','varchar(50)')   As
ClaimNumber
 ,CAST(SUBSTRING(pc.value('../DTP_SubLoop[1]/DTP_Statement-
Dates[1]/
  DTP03_StatementFromorToDate[1]','varchar(50)'),1,8)      As
Datetime)
  As SubmissionDate
 ,px2b.value('NM1_SubLoop_3[1]/TS837_2010BB_Loop[1]/NM1_Pay-
erName[1]/NM103_PayerName
  [1]','varchar(50)') as PayerName

FROM #xml
CROSS     APPLY     SOURCEDATA.nodes('//X12_00501_837_I')     AS
pheader(phead)
```

```
CROSS APPLY
phead.nodes('//TS837_2000A_Loop/TS837_2000B_Loop/TS837_2300_
Loop/
 CLM_Claiminformation') AS pClaim(pc)
CROSS APPLY phead.nodes('//TS837_2000B_Loop')as px2000B(px2b)
```

Oracle and XML

Just as SQL Server can be used to work natively with XML data, so too can Oracle. Eliminating the reliance of your orchestrations on any adapter that creates generated items or adds complexity in interactions with the source or target environments should be your key goal in your upgraded code. The Oracle adapter is no different – skip it and use C#.

For this example, the data is pulled from Oracle by the BizTalk orchestration via a C# assembly. The code shown in Listing 4.5 shows how to convert an Oracle record set into an XML formatted document. Figure 4.16 shows what the formatted XML from this SELECT query would look like.

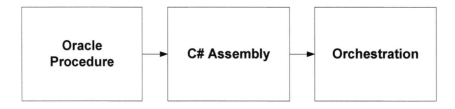

Figure 4.16 Example scenario pulls data from Oracle into an orchestration

Listing 4.5. Creating an XML result set in Oracle

```
    SELECT XMLElement("ResultsFor274",XMLAgg(
                    XMLElement("PROVIDER_GROUP"
                    ,XMLForest(    PROVNETWORKNAME As MAS-
TER_GROUP_CODE
                                ,GROUPTAXIDNUMBER As
TAX_ID
                                ,SUBSTR(PROVGRPNAME,1,59)
As IRS_NAME
                                ,ROWNUM As GROUPNUMBER
                                ,(SELECT COUNT(DISTINCT
SITENAME)
```

```
                                        FROM PROVIDER_NETWORK
PMAIN
                                        WHERE PMAIN.SITETAXONO-
MYCODE IS NOT NULL
                                        ) As SITECOUNT
                                      )
                                    )
                                  )
                                )

    FROM (  SELECT DISTINCT PROVNETWORKNAME,GROUPTAXID-
NUMBER,PROVGRPNAME
            FROM PROVIDER_NETWORK PMASTER
            WHERE GROUPTAXONOMYCODE IS NOT NULL
        ) PMASTER
```

```
  <?xml version="1.0"?>
- <ResultsFor274>
   - <PROVIDER_GROUP>
        <MASTER_GROUP_CODE>LIGHTHEALTH</MASTER_GROUP_CODE>
        <TAX_ID>888614888</TAX_ID>
        <IRS_NAME>Northern Valley Healthcare</IRS_NAME>
        <GROUPNUMBER>1</GROUPNUMBER>
        <SITECOUNT>1</SITECOUNT>
     </PROVIDER_GROUP>
   - <PROVIDER_GROUP>
        <MASTER_GROUP_CODE>MEDALERT</MASTER_GROUP_CODE>
        <TAX_ID>666516777</TAX_ID>
        <IRS_NAME>RALPH'S PHARMACY</IRS_NAME>
        <GROUPNUMBER>2</GROUPNUMBER>
        <SITECOUNT>1</SITECOUNT>
     </PROVIDER_GROUP>
  </ResultsFor274>
```

Figure 4.16: An example of the resulting XML document from Oracle

Revisiting WCF and SOAP Integrations

What has been said above about SQL and Oracle integrations is true for most of the more advanced adapters. Calls to WCF and SOAP services are very similar in nature when using the out-of-the-box options. Wizards will create schemas and ports automatically. Things can get extremely complex when dealing with services that have multiple endpoints or varied functionality. An example of an XSD that gets automatically generated from the WCF wizard within an orchestration can be seen in Figure 4.17.

Figure 4.17: XSD auto-generated by the BizTalk wizard

In turn, you should create a variety of ports and messages to communicate with your services. With one service within an orchestration, things can become unruly with these generated items. With many services, things can become virtually unusable. You should instead use the same approach described above for the SQL and Oracle adapters; namely, adding a C# class. This class then becomes the location where all the code used to interact with the service resides (see Figure 4.18).

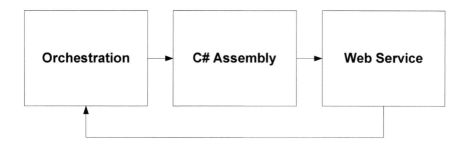

Figure 4.18: Flow for calling a web service

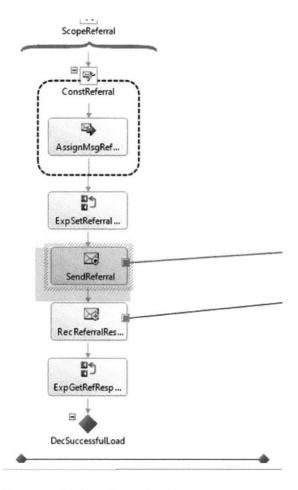

Figure 4.19: Flow for calling a web service

By programming your interaction with the web service in C#, you can take an orchestration that requires the multiple steps in Figure 4.19 to get a single value back from a service into the orchestration shown in Figure 4.20. The code for the revised approach is not extensive. Listing 4.6 gives an example of what the code could look like. In this code, an orchestration that was calling a SOAP web service directly is now calling the SOAP service through C#.

Listing 4.6. Calling the SOAP service through code called from the Expression shape

```
// following instantiates the service reference
FFACustomerProfileQuery.Port_ReceivePostData postFFACPQ =
new FFACustomerProfileQuery.Port_ReceivePostData();

FFACustomerProfileQuery.PostData reqFFACPQ = new
 FFACustomerProfileQuery.PostData();

FFACustomerProfileQuery.Response resFFACPQ = new
 FFACustomerProfileQuery.Response();

// set the input value

reqFFACPQ.CustomerID = "Value passed from Orchestration";

// set the URL and credentials (these would also be
// passed in from the orchestration, likely coming from the
configuration file)

postFFACPQ.Url   =   textBoxServer.Text   +   "/customerpro-
filequery_Proxy/
 Port_ReceivePostData.asmx";

System.Net.NetworkCredential cred = new
 NetworkCredential(_username, _password, _domain);

postFFACPQ.Credentials = cred;

// this performs the actual web service call

resFFACPQ = postFFACPQ.PostData(reqFFACPQ);

// this would be the value returned to the orchestration

resultValue = resFFACPQ.SuccessOrFailureMessage;
```

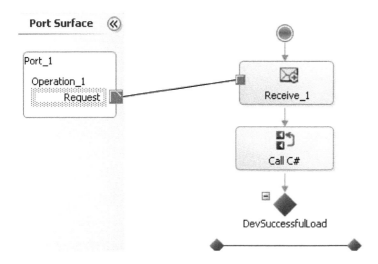

Figure 4.20: Flow for calling a web service

Summary

If your orchestrations are complex and difficult to migrate, take some time to re-think your approach with how they have been programmed. While it might take some work to redevelop them, you will save time in the testing and validation process. What you hopefully have gained from this chapter is that your best approach to BizTalk development is to avoid the heavyweight adapters and the generated items that come with them and rely instead on good programming practices that leverage the technologies available to you. Moving functionality from the orchestration into C# assemblies and the database tier not only can simplify your orchestrations, but will also make them perform more efficiently and be supportable by a wider range of developers.

Chapter 5
Migrating to Azure

There are two types of Azure solutions. The first is a "hosted server" model in which you rent servers hosted in the cloud and administrated through the Azure portal. The second model is "BizTalk Services," which are actual stand-alone Azure services that have similar functionality to some of the BizTalk on-premise processes, but are otherwise unrelated. In this chapter, we'll look at both models. What you will find is that with the hosted server model, you can migrate your existing solutions just as you would to any other new BizTalk 2016 environment, while with the BizTalk Services model, you are dealing with a completely different technology, one that will require a full rewrite of your components.

Hosted Azure Servers

There are many companies that offer to host servers (Rackspace, Microsoft, Amazon.com to name a few). These servers may be physical or virtual, and there will be different offerings with each. With Azure, the hosted servers are all virtual, and you must manage everything yourself, just as you would your own infrastructure. Everything is managed through the Microsoft Azure portal. Using this portal, you can create new virtual machines, set up disaster recovery, implement failover and web balancing, create backups, and a perform a wide variety of other activities.

There are companies that offer managed services for Azure environments. If you are dealing with a production environment of any complexity and you do not have an internal IT team, you may want to look into this. The cost is usually a percentage of what you spend on your Azure services.

The Azure portal has an extensive menu and a wide array of services and functionality. When you have virtual machines set up in Azure, the main dashboard can be customized to get a view into your server health, as shown in Figure 5.1. This dashboard will show performance and hardware usage without having to remote-desktop into any of your servers.

Hosting a server in Azure is just one of many services you can choose to implement within Azure. The Azure environment is constantly changing, and functionality is always being added and improved.

DOI 10.1515/9781501506086-005

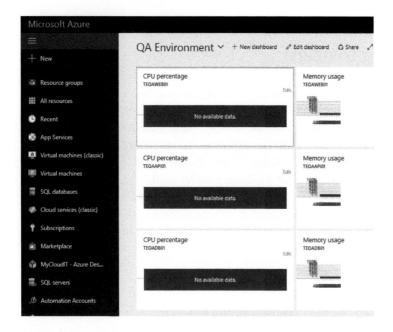

Figure 5.1: Main dashboard

From here, you can access any of your virtual machines, as shown in Figure 5.2. You can see status, IP addresses, and other top-level information about your servers from here.

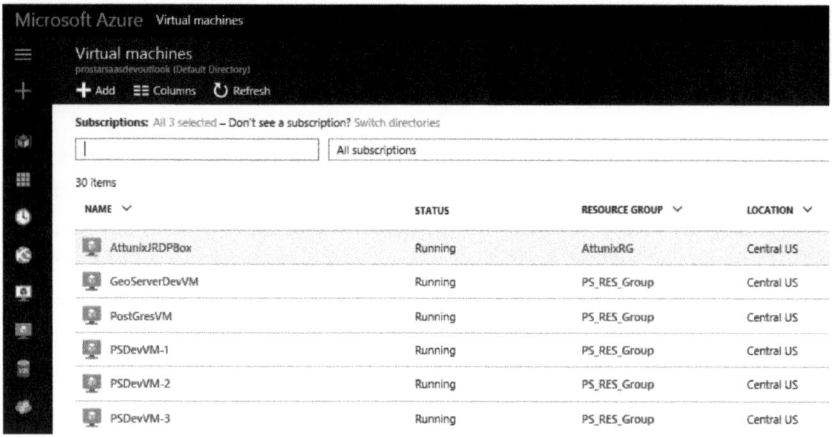

Figure 5.2: The Virtual Machine list

Clicking on any of these machines will give you extensive details about your specific machine, including the ability to remote-desktop into the environment (see Figure 5.3).

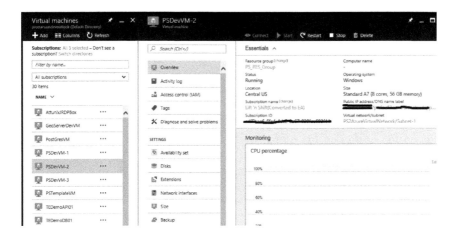

Figure 5.3: Functionality available on a single Azure VM instance

From an administrative point of view, Azure's dashboard, views, metrics, and functionality are enormously helpful. You don't have to search through each of your boxes; instead everything is rolled up and presented to you. Creating a similar view for an on-premise server environment would be a challenge.

Regarding the administration of the boxes themselves, you'll need to set up servers, apply patches, perform reboots, ensure that you are backing up your servers and data – in short, you'll have to do everything. With a small number of servers not in a production setting, this can be fairly simple, and you could set up your network in a short time. However, with many servers, your network can quickly become intricate and complex, and a healthy server environment can require a similar level of system administration that an on-premise set of servers would require.

An Azure-hosted virtual machine will have the same options available as a hosted server with virtually any other hosted-server provider. Your decision as to which provider to use will be based on price and functionality of the dashboards and related services (Rackspace, for example, provides full support via tickets and phone so that you don't have to deal with the core administration of the system.) The actual hosted-server environment will have identical options, and Biz-Talk can run in any of them – as an example, Figure 5.4 shows BizTalk running in an Amazon Web Services (AWS) hosted server.

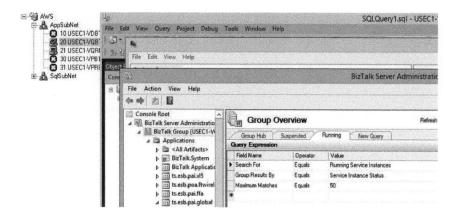

Figure 5.4: BizTalk running on an Amazon Web Services (AWS) hosted server

For the purposes of a BizTalk 2016 implementation within a hosted Azure model, you would need to set up new servers just as you would for an on-premise solution. Set up the servers (SQL and BizTalk), install and configure the media, and migrate your components, all exactly as has been outlined in Chapter 1 and 2 of this book. In fact, the only difference is how you will administer the VMs themselves (through Azure). The basic flow of the migration will look like this:

1. Start your Microsoft Azure Subscription.
2. Determine what your server architecture will be (single BizTalk Server, dual server with BizTalk and SQL, multiple BizTalk servers in a group, web server front end, etc.).
3. Create the virtual machines that you will need to support the server architecture you decide on from the previous step.
4. Install and configure your software (SQL and BizTalk).
5. Migrate your BizTalk solutions (as outlined in Chapter 2).

That's all there is to it. Azure-hosted servers really are the same as on-premise when it comes to a basic installation of BizTalk. You can even set up Azure to reside on your local network, and it will look just like any other server within your environment.

While hosted Azure servers may be virtually identical to an on-premise Biz-Talk solution, you'll now look at Azure BizTalk Services, which are similar in name only.

Azure BizTalk Services

Microsoft Azure has a wide variety of available services, one category of which is BizTalk Services. These services offer similar functionality to some aspects of the on-premise version of BizTalk, such as the ability to route and map data. In this section, we'll look at a specific migration scenario and walk through the steps to get it set up in Azure. What you will find is that you won't be migrating your existing on-premise components to BizTalk Services; rather, you will be developing new components for Azure that may be based on what you currently have in your on-premise solution.

Your MSDN account will have some level of credit available for you to work with Azure for free. However, you will need to closely manage this credit. You can see your credit status (see Figure 5.5). Azure can get expensive quickly, and there are many techniques for managing these costs. For purposes of this demo, you should have ample free credit to work through it.

Figure 5.5: Monitor your credit usage carefully with Azure

Developing and Deploying a BizTalk Azure Solution

The example that will be used for this discussion will be a simple model of moving a document from one FTP server to another. In this case, assume you have an on-premise solution that consists of the following components:
- Receive Port
- Receive Location that uses the FTP adapter to receive files on an FTP server

- Send Port with a filter subscribing to the data picked up on the Receive Port and using the FTP adapter to send the file to the destination

The BizTalk Service equivalent to this will be:
- FTP Source
- Pass-Through Bridge
- FTP Destination

We'll begin creating a BizTalk Service by signing in to the Azure portal and working through the following steps.

1. Using your MSDN account, log in to the Azure portal. There are two portals, and currently BizTalk Services is available only from the classic portal, which you can access at https://manage.windowsazure.com.
2. Click the giant "NEW" button at the bottom left of the portal screen and select App Services followed by BizTalk Service and then Custom Create, as shown in Figure 5.6.

Figure 5.6: Creating a new BizTalk Service in the classic portal

If you wish to access them via the new portal, you most likely will need to search for BizTalk and then select BizTalk Services (as shown in Figure 5.7). Clicking on this will give you a description and a Create button, which will link you back to the Classic portal options.

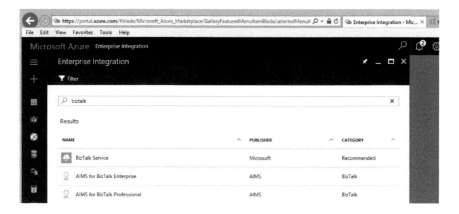

Figure 5.7: Locating BizTalk Services in the new Azure portal

3. On the Create BizTalk Service page, give your service a name, select an edition, and give a region, as shown in Figure 5.8. The BizTalk Service being created is a shell where you will be able to deploy a specific solution, as you will see in later steps.

NEW BIZTALK SERVICE – CUSTOM CREATE

Create BizTalk Service

BIZTALK SERVICE NAME

| demoservice | ! | .biztalk.windows.net ? |

EDITION

| Developer ∨ | ? |

REGION

| East US ∨ |

DOMAIN URL

| demoservice.biztalk.windows.net | ? |

Figure 5.8: Create a new BizTalk Service

4. Each BizTalk Service you create will run against its own storage account and database. On the second page of the service creation, you will need to name your storage account, as shown in Figure 5.9, followed by the settings for the specific database instance, as shown in Figure 5.10.

NEW BIZTALK SERVICE – CUSTOM CREATE

Storage and Database Configuration

MONITORING/ARCHIVING STORAGE ACCOUNT

Create a new storage account

STORAGE ACCOUNT NAME

demostorageinotek

TRACKING DATABASE

Create a new SQL Database instance

Figure 5.9: First page of the database configuration for the new BizTalk Service

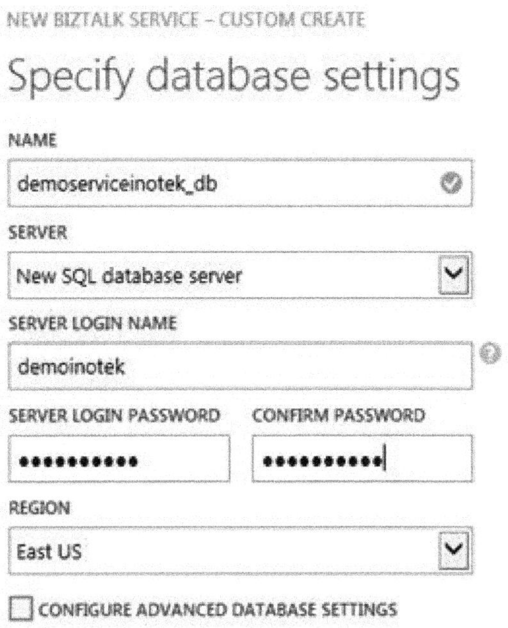

NEW BIZTALK SERVICE – CUSTOM CREATE

Specify database settings

NAME

| demoserviceinotek_db | ✓ |

SERVER

| New SQL database server | ∨ |

SERVER LOGIN NAME

| demoinotek | ⓘ |

SERVER LOGIN PASSWORD   CONFIRM PASSWORD

| •••••••••• | | •••••••••• |

REGION

| East US | ∨ |

☐ CONFIGURE ADVANCED DATABASE SETTINGS

Figure 5.10: Final page of the BizTalk Service configuration, specifying the DB Settings

With these steps completed, you will have a new BizTalk Service where you can deploy your solutions. Developing a solution is done in Visual Studio on your local machine, and then deployed to the cloud. The next set of steps outlines what you will need to do to develop and deploy a Visual Studio solution.

1. Before you can develop anything in Visual Studio, you will need to download the BizTalk Services SDK. This can be done via the Azure classic portal by clicking on the new BizTalk Service you created in the previous steps. When you click on it, you will see the option to Download BizTalk Services SDK located under Get the tools, as shown in Figure 5.11. Download the file (you will have 32-bit and 64-bit options) and install it on your machine.

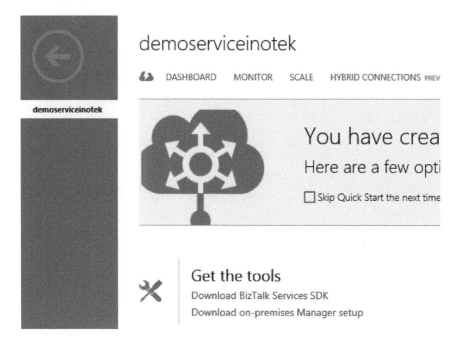

Figure 5.11: Download the SDK from the portal

2. With the SDK installed, you can open Visual Studio and create a new project. You will see BizTalk Services under the Visual C# templates, as shown in Figure 5.12.

Figure 5.12: Selecting the BizTalk Service template in Visual Studio

3. The template will create a new Project with a BCS file in it. This BCS file is where you will build out your flow for this example. Figure 5.13 shows a new project with the BCS file selected.

Figure 5.13: The BCS file in the new BizTalk project

4. Next, drag an FTP Source component from the Toolbox and drop it on the canvas of the opened BCS file. Right-click the newly dropped component, and set the properties, as shown in Figure 5.14. For the properties shown, this will pick up all files that have a TXT extension from the FTP server. You can, of course, set these however is appropriately for what you are doing.

Figure 5.14: Final page of the BizTalk Service configuration, specifying the DB Settings

5. Now, select a Pass-Through Bridge from the Toolbox (see Figure 5.15) and drop it to the right of the FTP Source. This bridge will perform no data validation on the data being transferred between the FTP sites. If you wanted to pass an XML doc and perform mapping on it, you would use the Xml One-Way Bridge, so that BizTalk could do schema resolution and mapping against the document.

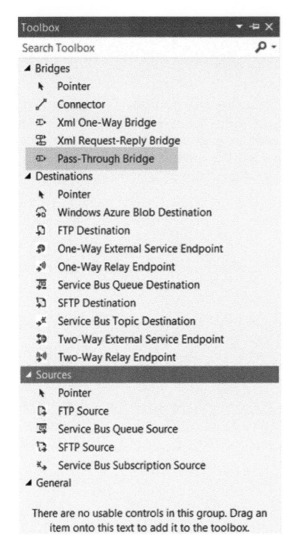

Figure 5.15: The Toolbox showing the BizTalk components

6. Place an FTP Destination shape to the right of the Bridge you just added. Right-click this to set the properties.
7. Add a connector to connect each of the shapes to each other. Your final flow should look similar to Figure 5.16.

FTPSource1   PassThroughBrid...   FTPDestination1

Figure 5.16: The shapes connected together

8. Double-click the Pass-Through Bridge shape and click on the Enrich box, as shown in Figure 5.17. This will allow you to open the properties and select Add, as shown in Figure 5.18.

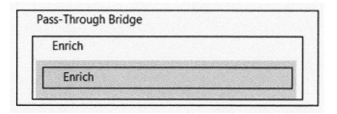

Pass-Through Bridge

Enrich

Enrich

Figure 5.17: Working with the Bridge settings

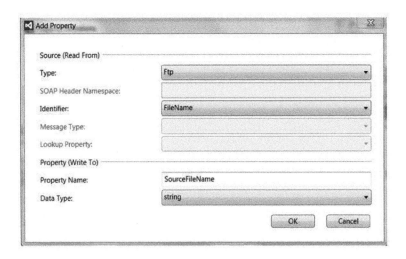

Figure 5.18: Access the properties of the Enrich shape

9. Back on the main BCS canvas, double-click the connector line that connects to the FTP Destination. Within the properties, set the filter to match all, as shown in Figure 5.19. This will allow all files to pass through.

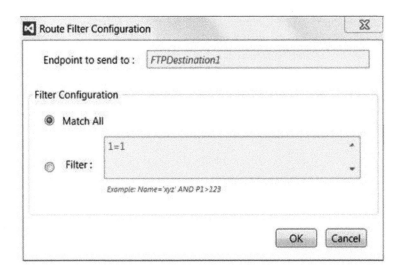

Figure 5.19: Allow all files to flow through to the FTP Destination

10. After clicking OK on the previous item, select the Route Action and pick Add. The settings shown in Figure 5.20 will set the target file name to the source file name.

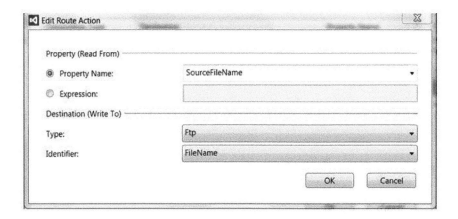

Figure 5.20: Setting the target name based on the source file name

11. You are now ready to deploy the solution to Azure. Save your BCS file and project and then right-click the project and select Deploy.
12. There are several things you will need to get from the Azure portal. The first is the SSL certificate. You can download this via the Download SSL Certificate link on your BizTalk Service's Dashboard page (bottom right), as shown in Figure 5.21. This certificate needs to be added to the Trusted Root certificates on your local machine. This can be done by typing MMC on your start menu. In the application that opens, click the File menu and select Add/Remove Snap In. From here, select Certificates, select Computer account, then click Finish. You can import your certificate from this final page.

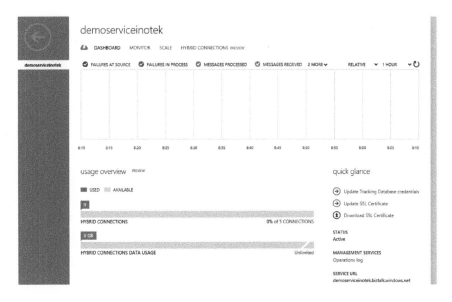

Figure 5.21: Download the SSL Certificate

13. The next thing you must do before deployment is get the service URL. This can be retrieved from your Azure portal in the bottom right, just below where the SSL Certificate download option was. The property name is Service URL, and this needs to be copied and pasted into the Deployment Endpoint in your deployment dialogue box (see first property in Figure 5.22).

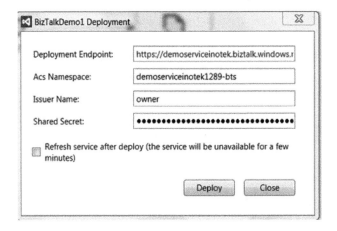

Figure 5.22: The deployment properties are set based on data from the Azure portal

14. Finally, click on the Connection Information button at the very bottom of your Azure Portal. This information (in Figure 5.23) must be copied and pasted into the remaining fields in the deployment box.

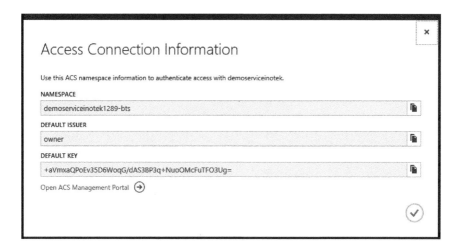

Figure 5.23: Access Connection Information needed for deployment

15. You should now be able to complete the deployment of your solution from Visual Studio to Azure by clicking the Deploy button. This will place the solution in your BizTalk Service in Azure.

Starting Your BizTalk Service

Unfortunately, the care and maintenance of BizTalk Services requires scripting. This section outlines how to start the service using PowerShell. You will need to begin by running the following commands from a Windows PowerShell script prompt (you can type PowerShell within your Windows Start menu to open the PowerShell tool).

import-module "C:\Program Files\Windows Azure BizTalk Services Tools\Microsoft.BizTalk.Services.Powershell.dll"

get-command -module Microsoft.BizTalk.Services.PowerShell

After these have executed, you will need to run a final one that has dynamic values in it. The parameters are based on what you've already retrieved from the Azure portal for the deployment. The values are:
- $acsns is the name of your BizTalk Service
- $in is the owner name from the Azure Connection Information properties
- $ik is the secret key, also from the Connection Information
- $du is the URL, which you set in the deployment options above

As shown in Figure 5.24, the following command can be executed in a series of statements within the PowerShell script tool.

```
Get-AzureBizTalkBridge –AcsNamespace $acsns -IssuerName
$in -IssuerKey $ik –DeploymentUri $du
```

Figure 5.24: Getting the Azure Bridge through PowerShell

You can verify the status of your bridge using the following command. This command's parameters indicate that the status is "False," which means it is stopped (see Figure 5.25).

```
Get-AzureBizTalkBridgeSource –AcsNamespace $acsns -IssuerName
$in -IssuerKey $ik –DeploymentUri $du -bridgepath PassThroughBridge1
```

```
PS C:\Users\Triston A> Get-AzureBizTalkBridgeSource -AcsNamespace $acsns -IssuerName $in -IssuerKey $ik -DeploymentUri $
du -bridgepath PassThroughBridge1

Name         : FTPSource1
Status       : False
Address      : https://demoserviceinotek.biztalk.windows.net/default/PassThroughBridge1/sources/FTPSource1
SourceType   : ftp
ServerAddress : 72.167.2.128
ServerPort   : 21
BridgePath   : PassThroughBridge1
```

Figure 5.25: Verifying the status of the bridge

You can issue a start command, as follows, to start the process.

```
Start-AzureBizTalkBridgeSource –AcsNamespace $acsns -IssuerName
$in –IssuerKey $ik –DeploymentUri $du –BridgePath PassThroughBridge1
```

You should now be able to drop a file on your FTP site where the FTP Source is
pointing, and see it delivered to the FTP Destination.

Monitoring Your Azure BizTalk Service

Debugging and troubleshooting your BizTalk Service can be a challenge. You will
need to be aware of the logs available in Azure. In order to access, open the Azure
Portal and click on your BizTalk Services. Next, click the Manage button at the
bottom of the screen (see Figure 5.26). This will open a new window where you
can click on the Tracking button. From here, all the log details for any of your
deployed services will show here. You can click on an item and then select the
"Details" button, available at the bottom of the window (shown in Figure 5.27).

Figure 5.26: Click the Manage button from this screen

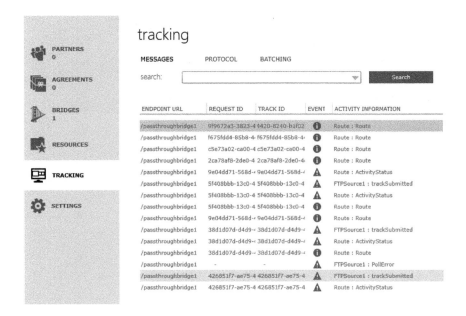

Figure 5.27: Seeing the status of processes within the Tracking dashboard

You also will want to connect to the database you created during the setup of the BizTalk Service. This database is accessible via the database menu option in the Azure portal, as shown in Figure 5.28.

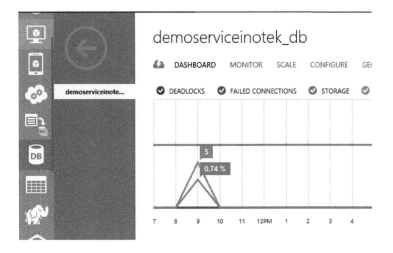

Figure 5.28: A SQL Azure database is created during the BizTalk Service creation

You can connect to a SQL Azure database just as you would to a local. The connection information is under the "quick glance" of the SQL dashboard, as shown in Figure 5.29.

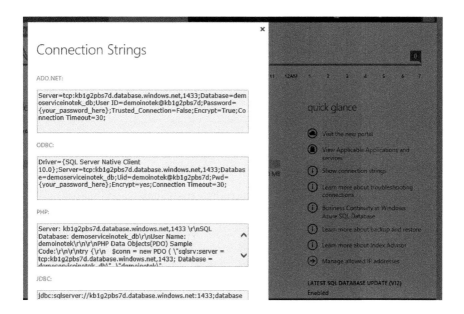

Figure 5.29: Connection strings

Taking the connection information, you can connect using SQL Server Management Studio (see Figure 5.30). You will likely have to set up firewall access between your Azure SQL and your local machine before you'll be able to connect. Once you are connected, you'll be able to query the database and get information about your running BizTalk Services.

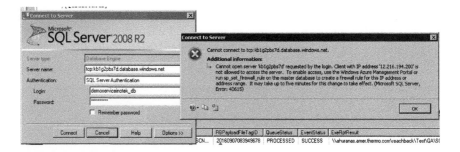

Figure 5.30: Connecting to Azure SQL will require setting rules with the Portal to allow external connections

Summary

There are two models of BizTalk in Azure. The first is the hosted model, which is identical to an on-premise installation of BizTalk, except that it is a hosted server. The second is Azure BizTalk Services, which are a completely separate entity from on-premise solutions. With the hosted model, you can migrate your components to an Azure server, just as you would any other server. With the BizTalk Services, you would have to write code from scratch – there is no migration of existing solutions.

Since BizTalk Services will require that you rewrite your components, you should first look at all of the functionality available to you through the wide variety of other Azure services. You'll need to architect things properly for Azure Services, and BizTalk Services is just one of wide array of options.

Appendix
Managing Your Migration

You hold in your hands all the technical details you require for a successful Biz-Talk Migration. This appendix is designed to show you one way of managing the effort, capturing and assigning the tasks, and showing your progress. Team Foundation Server (TFS) and its Azure-based counterpart, Visual Studio Team Services (VSTS), are one of those rare gems almost never seen outside development teams. This is unfortunate as TFS (also known as VSTS) is one of the best tools we have encountered for managing technical projects – even those like a BizTalk Migration that may require little or no code development.

As a technical project management tool – or in Microsoft parlance, an Application Lifecycle Management (ALM) platform – TFS is flexible, adaptive, and widely supported. Whether you are a Waterfall, SCRUM/Agile, LEAN, or all of the above shop, TFS was designed to fit your operational style as opposed to dictating a particular approach. In this case, we have a code-free, almost entirely infrastructure-based project that in today's world might be called "DevOps."

Creating a TFS Project

Unless your Dev team already has TFS, the first thing you will need to do is get an instance of TFS up and running. You can begin this with a Free Visual Studio Team Service account at https://www.visualstudio.com/team-services/. As this book goes to press the Visual Studio Team Services home page has a prominent "Get started for free" button that opens the following page as seen in Figure A.1.

Start by giving your account a name. You can click on the "Get started for free" button within the VSTS home page to get to the screen shown in Figure A.1.

DOI 10.1515/9781501506086-006

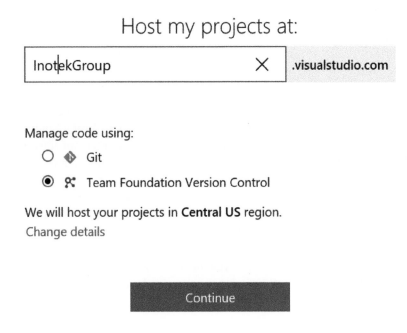

Figure A.1: Creating a new account

Clicking Continue is all that is required to create the instance. You now have TFS available to your organization. Now that you have TFS up and running, or with this book in hand you convinced your dev manager to let you in on the TFS magic, you will want to capture your BizTalk Migration effort in a TFS project. What you choose to name your first project is dependent on how you plan to use TFS going forward.

If your BizTalk Migration is part of a larger project and largely managed by your Infrastructure team it might be best to name your project "Infrastructure" and add your BizTalk Migration as a Project work item under it. For illustration purposes we will accept the default "MyFirstProject," which we will change later. In Figure A.2 you can see the start page for your new project.

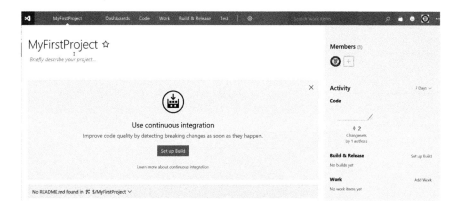

Figure A.2: Creating a new project

TFS splits its navigation into TFS Administration and Project Administration. The Administrative navigation is available via the Settings gear as shown in Figure A.3.

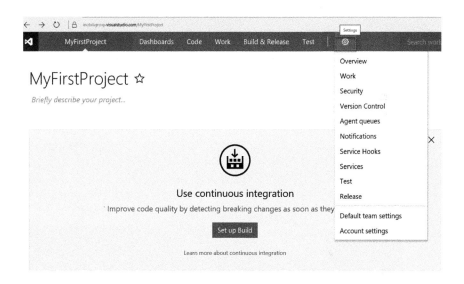

Figure A.3: The Settings menu

The Project navigation is available via the header menu and the left-hand project menu. Bring up the project menu by hovering over the Visual Studio icon in the upper left corner as shown in Figure A.4.

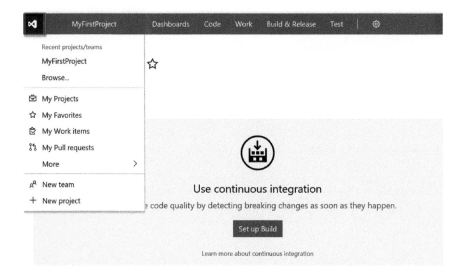

Figure A.4: The project menu

Clicking on the Visual Studio icon in the upper left will take you to the Projects landing page shown in Figure A.5.

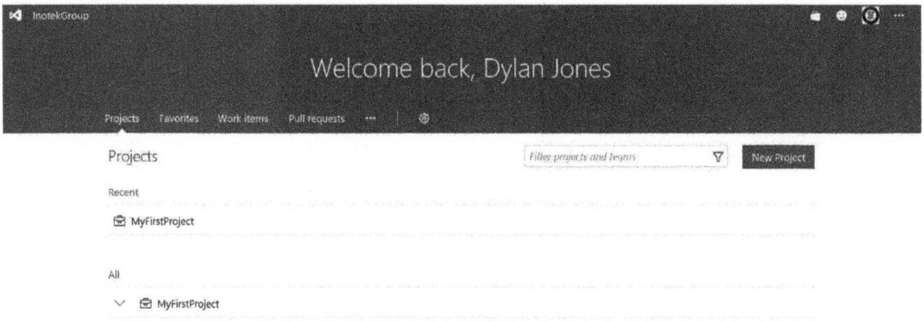

Figure A.5: The project-landing page

As your first task, open "MyFirstProject" and rename it. To accomplish this, open the project by clicking on the project link ("MyFirstProject") as shown above in Figure A.5. Either the one listed under Recent or the one under all will work. Once the Project page is displayed, use the Settings gear as shown in Figure A.6 to select the Account Settings option. Clicking this will bring you to the Project Admin Overview page.

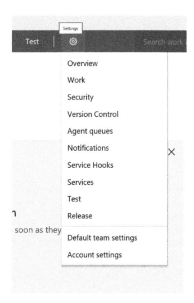

Figure A.6: Select the Account Settings option

Select the ellipses (...) next to "MyFirstProject" and select Rename, as shown in Figure A.7. Rename your project something like "BizTalk Migration." At this point we should take some time to discuss a few important points that you should be aware off. The first is the process template used for your project. TFS comes with three process templates, which mainly differ by work-item types.

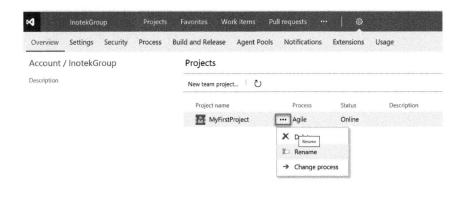

Figure A.7: Renaming the project

Agile, CMMI, and Scrum

Chances are if you don't have TFS in your environment already that your organization is not practicing Application Lifecyle Management as described by Microsoft. However, your development team may be an Agile or Scrum shop, have had extensive training and have implemented one of these methodologies, and the business side of your organization is at least familiar with it. If that is the case, you may want to pick the Agile or Scrum template. If you do, understand that you must forego risk and change management, as well as hours of tracking, which I have found are often very useful for projects involving infrastructure. But, if your organization does not strictly adhere to any one methodology or you have the flexibility, I think you will find the CMMI template to be most familiar to your audience and lends itself to both LEAN thinking and codeless projects like a BizTalk Migration. The grid in Figure A.8 outlines the work-item type support under each template.

Work Item Type (WIT)	Agile	CMMI	Scrum
EPIC	●	●	●
Feature	●	●	●
Requirement		●	
Product backlog item			●
User Story	●		
Bug	●	●	●
Task	●	●	●
Impediment			●
Issue	●	●	
Change Request		●	
Review		●	
Risk		●	

Figure A.8: Work items supported under each type of project

While the selection of a template can involve an emotional debate in which adherents of a methodology or framework will engage in a red-faced debate, do yourself a favor and sidestep all this by picking the one you're comfortable with. You can always migrate to another template later. For infrastructure-related projects I have found the CMMI template to be a good fit. In fact, I have found CMMI to be a great fit regardless of methodology, and I like that it allows hours to be assigned to tasks I have found to be the easiest and most widely accepted measure of effort across teams.

Let's change the process template to CMMI. Click the Agile link you saw back in Figure A.7. This will open the Process description page, which is another source of information on each process. Hover over the Settings gear and select the Default Settings option. Once the page has refreshed, hover over the Settings gear again and select Project Settings. This will open the Project profile page. The current process is listed under Process, which is also the location that we will use to change the process template to CMMI (see Figure A.9).

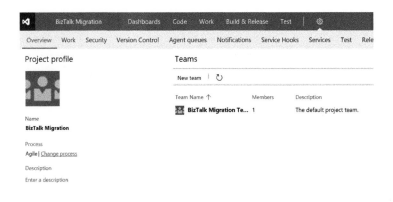

Figure A.9: Project profile shows the type of process (currently set to Agile)

If you find yourself unable to change the process of an existing project, you can always delete it and create a new one. To do so click on the Projects menu. Create new project is the default view, as shown in Figure A.10. Enter the project name, select the Version Control (Git or Team Foundation Version Control), and choose one of the three Work item process templates.

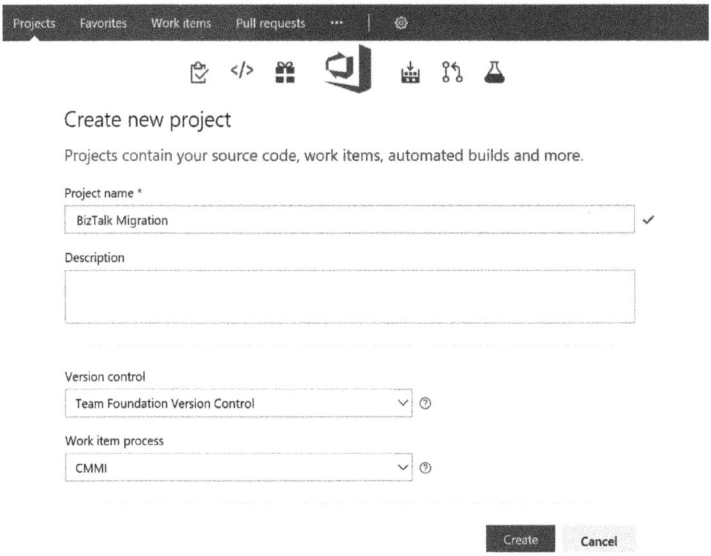

Figure A.10: Starting over on the project naming

Features, Requirements, and Tasks

Now that you have TFS setup and your project configured, the goal is to represent the project work within TFS. The following list is a high-level outline of a sample BizTalk Migration effort. We'll use these to model out our project work.

1. Plan the deployment activities
   a. Architecture
   b. Migrate BizTalk components
   c. Migrate non-BizTalk components
2. BizTalk installation
   a. Prepare core servers
   b. Install SQL
   c. Install and configure BizTalk
3. Visual Studio
   a. Recompile BizTalk projects to upgrade to latest version
4. Manual deployment activities
   a. Deploy BizTalk assemblies
5. Automatic deployment activities
   a. Export MSI
   b. Export Binding files
   c. Import MSI
   d. Import Binding files
6. Testing
   a. Test maps
7. Test end to end solutions

Start by adding the numbered items as Features. Click the Dashboard menu item, as shown in Figure A.11. This will open the Overview dashboard (see Figure A.12). This overview dashboard is standard to all projects and, as you learn more about TFS, you may opt to add additional dashboards. At this point the overview dashboard is sufficient.

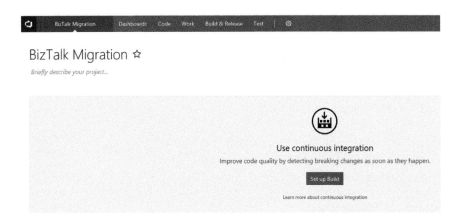

Figure A.11: The dashboard menu

Figure A.12: The overview dashboard

At the top of the Welcome box is a Manage Work link click that and you will be presented with the Backlog Kanban board. At this point, nothing is present, as you have not entered any items. Select the Features item as shown in the top left corner of Figure A.13.

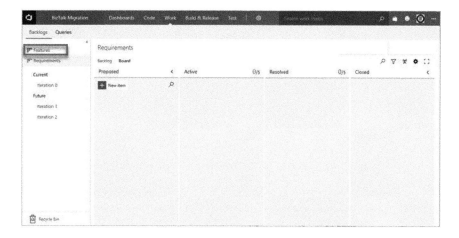

Figure A.13: Click the Features menu item

Now select the Backlog option shown in Figure A.14.

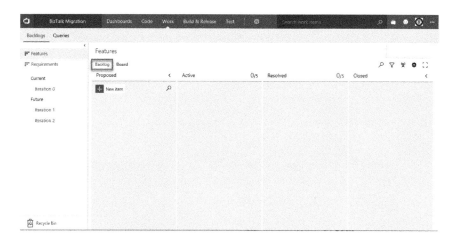

Figure A.14: Selecting the Backlog option

You are presented with a Backlog for features and can enter the titles (see Figure A.15). Complete this process for each of the items listed in the outline of work given earlier in this section.

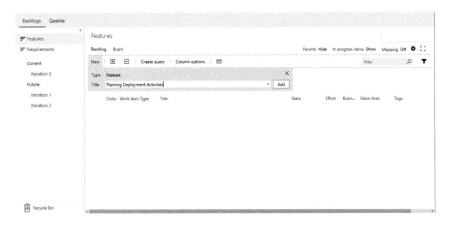

Figure A.15: Creating features

As you add each Feature you will see the backlog begin to populate with the Features you add (see Figure A.16). Follow the same process you did for each Feature by adding each requirement until your backlog is complete.

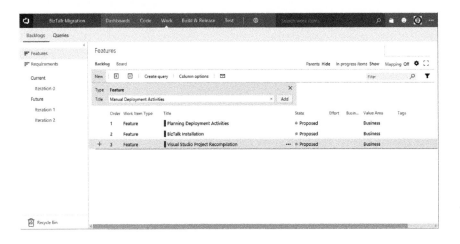

Figure A.16: Features being populated

Once you have all the features entered, select the Requirements link in left-hand menu, as shown in Figure A.17.

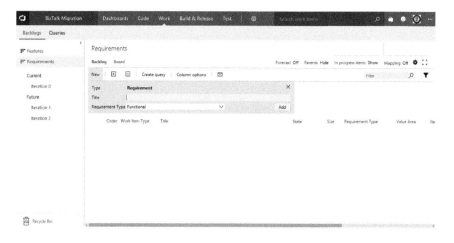

Figure A.17: Creating a Requirement

Similar to the Feature entry, you will create all your Requirements (refer back to the work list from the beginning of this section). You will then want to map each Requirement to its respective Feature. To do this, click on the "Mapping Off" indicator to turn mapping on as shown in Figure A.18.

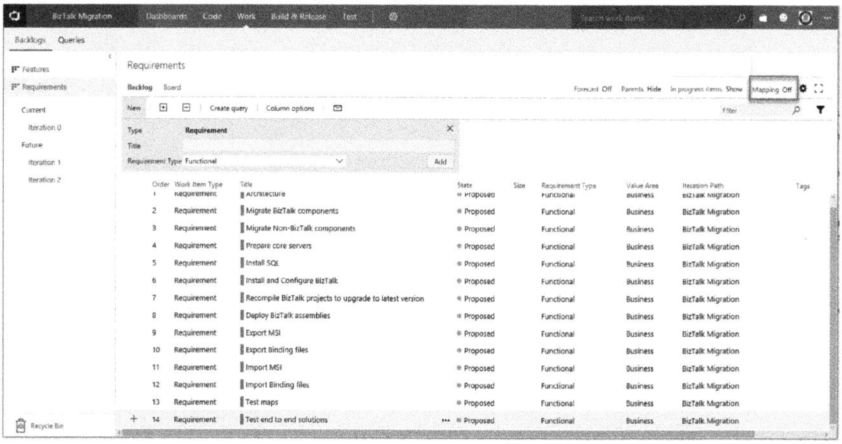

Figure A.18: Turn mapping on by clicking the "Mapping Off" option in the upper right hand corner

When you have turned mapping on, all the features in your backlog will appear on the left-hand sign of the page as shown in Figure A.19. You can map the requirements to the features simply by dragging and dropping each Requirement onto the appropriate Feature.

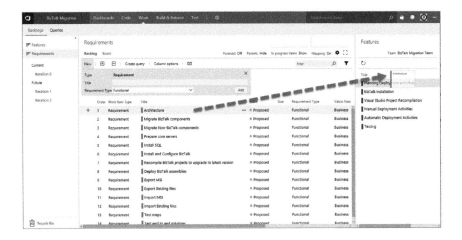

Figure A.19: Mapping requirements to features

After the mapping of Requirements to Features has been completed, click on the Features link under backlogs and then the expand on level "+" icon to display the Feature \ Requirement hierarchy of your backlog, as shown in Figure A.20.

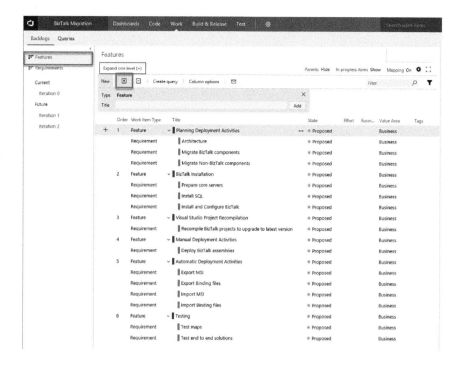

Figure A.20: The Features and Requirements hierarchy

As a final step, you will want to add the Tasks to be taken to meet each requirement. To add Tasks, select the appropriate requirement, click the plus sign next
to it and then click Add data (see Figure A.21).

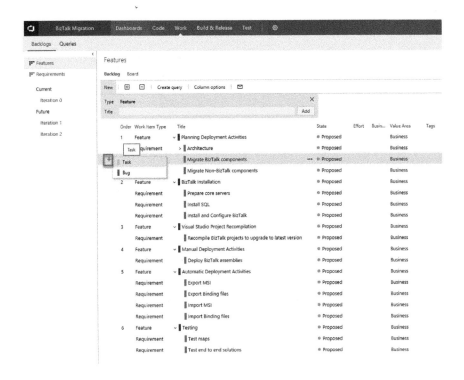

Figure A.21: Adding a Task

The Add Task dialog window will display. Enter a title for the Task, provide a description, attach any associated documents and provide an estimate of hours. Figure A.22 shows a Task being entered.

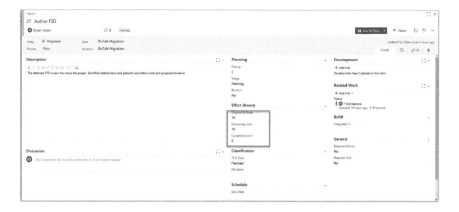

Figure A.22: Creating the Task

Unless you have added members to your project team the Task is assigned to you by default, as you are currently the active team member. Unless you're doing all the work yourself, you will want to add new members to your team. To add new members, return to the project root (you can refer to Figure A.4 earlier in the chapter), then open the administrative navigation (also shown earlier in Figure A.6) and select Security. This will open the Security landing page. Select your Team (BizTalk Migration Team) on the left, select Members, Add, and then enter the email or user name in the Search users and groups text area (see Figure A.23). Save your changes when complete.

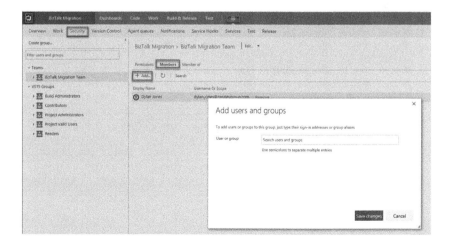

Figure A.23: Adding additional users

Create your next Task and select the user who should complete the work and save your Task (see Figure A.24).

Figure A.24: Assigning tasks to users

Eventually, you will have entered all the tasks related to the requirements, and you can now plan and execute on your work. Figure A.25 displays the completed Requirements backlog.

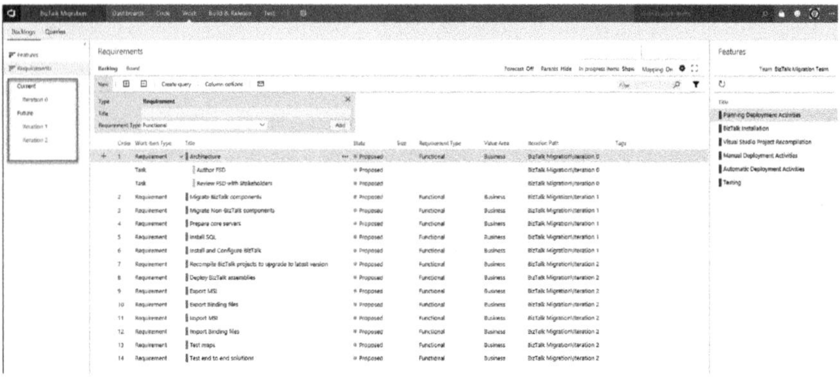

Figure A.25: The completed backlog

In the left column is the list of iterations for your team. Each iteration represents a two-week period. Your job is to drag and drop each requirement onto the two-week period that represents when the work will be started. Once this is complete you can view the Task Board and drag Tasks into the active column as you start them. When the Task is completed, drag it to Resolved. Once the item has passed its review or test, drag it to the closed column. Figure A.26 shows the board where items can be dragged and dropped to set status.

Figure A.26: The board view

Summary

We have presented the bare bones necessary to manage your BizTalk Migration using TFS. We have touched only the surface of the capabilities and features present in the application. Regardless of the tool you use, it is very important that you manage the project. Having your work effort outlined and mapped out is critical not only for your own sanity, but also benefits your team and, as important, your customer.

Index